CA$H

FOR THE

FINAL DAYS

CA$H

FOR THE

FINAL DAYS

A Financial Guide for the Terminally Ill and Their Advisors

Gloria Grening Wolk

Forward by Ralph Nader

BIALKIN BOOKS
LAGUNA HILLS, CALIFORNIA

 First edition published by Bialkin Books, 25381 Alicia Pkwy, #G-336, Laguna Hills, California 92653.

Warning — Disclaimer

Quotes from viatical providers were chosen for suitability to text, and do not represent an endorsement of any individual or firm.

P-CIP Data

Wolk, Gloria Grening

Cash for the final days : a financial guide for the terminally ill and their advisors / by Gloria Grening Wolk.

p. cm.

Includes bibliographical references and index.

LCCN: 96-96464

ISBN 0-9652615-3-0

1. Terminally ill--Finance, Personal. 2. Patients--Finance, Personal. 3. Insurance, Life--Policies. 4. Estate planning. I. Title

HG179.W65 1996 332.024'0814

QBI96-40131

Cover Design: White Light Publishing, Huntington Beach, CA

Copy Editor: Shirl Thomas

ACKNOWLEDGEMENTS

This is a wonderful opportunity to pay tribute to the staff, volunteers, and clients of AIDS Services Foundation. Through their combined efforts, ASF has become a cheerful place as well as an oasis of goodness and caring.

Many ASF clients contributed to this book, but I am equally indebted to many others — some of whom are gone now — for the warmth, sincerity and openness that greatly enriched my life.

It was my good fortune to be the beneficiary of the knowledge and experience of three advocates for the terminally ill: the late David Peterson, founder of New York-based Affording Care, who continued to educate and inform almost to the day of his death in May, 1996; Per Larson, a New York-based financial advisor and advocate for the terminally ill; and Thomas McCormack of Washington, D.C., author of "The AIDS Benefit Handbook."

Attorney Dave McDowell of Laguna Hills offered such valuable estate planning advice that I revised Chapter 9 to include his ideas. Neighbor and fellow dog-lover, Mark Welch, C.P.A., took time from his busy schedule to review the sections that relate to his area of expertise. Harold Prommell, of the National Writers Association Press, and Diane Stelley, of the critique committee of the Southern California chapter of NWA, generously shared their knowledge about publishing and writing. Mitch Lucio, a computer-whiz friend, undertook the design of the Universal Application and Authorization forms, after learning that in my frenzy to get the book done quickly, I contemplated abandoning plans to include the forms.

I shall forever be grateful to long-term friends whose moral support sustained me over the years. On the east coast, they are: Roberta and Bernie Bernhardt, Dilshad (Candy) and Anand Bhatia, Geraldine and John Esposito, Lorrie and Dave Jorsey, Bill Odoy, C.P.A. (whose gratuitous advice benefitted ASF clients), Leanne and Ballie Singh and, much farther east, Kiwako Yuba of Osaka, Japan, a devoted friend for nearly thirty years.

Mary BonAmi Chutjian, another long-time friend and possibly the only person who has read nearly everything I ever published, used these past achievements to encourage me (and, I suspect, to feed her unwavering optimism).

Since relocating to the Golden State, I've been blessed with equally wonderful friends: Kathleen Karls, Eric Culverson, Glenna Keating, and Bara Salman. I've no doubt they will pooh-pooh their significance to my well-being, as people who give freely are apt to do.

Of all my new-found friends, Christopher Miller had the most profound effect. He approached me one day, as my German Shepherd and I set out on our morning walk. He asked to join us, explaining that he was stuck at home on disability, that he was depressed, that he needed an excuse to get out and exercise. Soon we were friends. Then good friends. And, in the months left to him, Chris led me to the door of his world and inspired me to become a volunteer at AIDS Services Foundation.

In Memory of Christopher Miller

forever 33

"When we walk our way and encounter a man who comes toward us, walking his way, we know our way only and not his; for his comes to life for us only in the encounter."

— Martin Buber, *I and Thou*

ABOUT THE AUTHOR

Gloria Grening Wolk has been a financial services professional since 1984, is licensed for life and health insurance as well as tax preparation, and has taught financial planning courses for adult education programs.

Her undergraduate degree was earned at the City College of New York, and the Master's degree in Social Work from the University of Connecticut. For the past several years Gloria Wolk has provided pro bono tax and other financial services to clients of AIDS Services Foundation, Orange county, California. This book is an outgrowth of those experiences.

Clients mentioned throughout the book are real, as are their questions and problems. However, with the exception of Christopher Miller, no actual names have been used.

FOREWORD

"You have less than a year to live," the doctor tells you. As you struggle to deal with this news, the doctor and hospital bills are pouring in. It may be impossible to keep working. You wonder, "How can I handle these bills? How can I keep afloat?"

When people are very ill and under extreme pressure to pay mounting doctor and hospital bills, they are vulnerable to any pitch promising them fast financial relief.

Viatical settlements were created with a promise to get cash into the hands of these very ill people. Viatical settlements are contracts in which a terminally ill person gets cash in exchange for turning over the death benefits in that person's life insurance policy to the person supplying the cash. Sometimes the deals struck are fair. Often, however, far too much of the death benefit goes into the hands of those offering the Viatical Settlement contracts.

If ever there was a need for some regulation of behavior, it is in the area of Viatical Settlement dealings. But far too few states have enacted legislation to protect the terminally ill from those who would rip them off in their vulnerable state. Unfortunately, far too frequently the only person standing between these sharp dealers who would rob the dying and the terminally ill person is *the terminally ill person*.

This is why Gloria Wolk wrote this book. The word must get out to the dying about their options and ways to assure a fair arrangement if a Viatical Settlement is the right option.

Until this book, there was no guide for the terminally ill and their loved ones through the maze of the Viatical Settlement industry; no way to maximize the cash going to the ill person;

no help in making the decision of whether to use Viatical Settlements at all; no discussion of other options for cash available to a very ill person.

Gloria Wolk has filled that void with this useful book. She leads the reader through the basics of Viatical Settlements, tells us who the players are (some, you'll learn, are not so nice), how to apply for a Viatical Settlement, explains how to maximize the amount of money you get, warns of what the tax consequences are, and itemizes other things to consider before entering into any Viatical Settlement contract. The book is an easy to understand, step-by-step approach to protect yourself when you need money near the end of life.

If you are a terminally ill person who needs money, or if you know a terminally ill person in that situation, you should read this book. Do not deal with a Viatical Settlement company or broker without reading this book!

Also, please write to your state legislator and tell the legislator to support legislation to regulate the Viatical Settlement industry. We cannot stand by and let the most vulnerable people in our society be victimized any longer.

Ralph Nader

PREFACE

This book began at AIDS Services Foundation, Orange county, California. For the past five years I've assisted ASF clients with tax preparation and advocacy, and advised them — sometimes through their caseworkers — about other financial concerns. Nearly two years ago Amy Canter, a Benefits Counselor, asked about the taxation of viatical settlements. Within weeks similar questions were posed by clients. I wasn't stumped by the questions, but it was foreseeable that I would be, in time: viatical settlements were becoming increasingly popular. Thus, I set out to learn everything about viatical settlements.

The quest began, logically enough, at the public library. After keying into the computer every possible word combination, I sat dumbfounded. Not one reference book existed anywhere. Newspapers and magazines offered a smattering of information: basic facts, a scam or two, and the concensus among journalists that this was a grisly, ghoulish business.

Having exhausted library resources, I turned to the California Department of Insurance (DOI). The DOI sent me a list of viatical providers permitted to transact business within the state. I phoned every provider, interviewed them, took copious notes, and requested application kits. One day, as my fingers trotted down the list, they stumbled upon what appeared to be the front organization for an unlicensed, illegal company. Alarmed, I notified the DOI, then asked the directors at AIDS Services Foundation to refer all queries about viatical settlements to me. My intention was to warn clients, but almost immediately I began educating them, as well.

How could I not? I had discovered a method to greatly increase the amount of their viatical settlements. Clients reported back: the method worked. The smallest extra (for a small life insurance policy) was $3,200. The largest extra (for a large policy) was $57,400.

They were happy to keep me informed, knowing I would use their experiences to help others. But when they phoned, their voices were laden with anxiety or fatigue. The viatical process exhausted them. Several felt tempted to leap at the first offer — just to get it over. And this taught me something else:

Clients need more than practical information: They need emotional support. They need family and friends to become involved, to help shoulder the burden, to remind them that it is a Seller's Market, and they need not take any guff.

Another discovery came when I sought advice from accountants and attorneys. Scarcely any knew what I was talking about. Some had spoken to clients who had sold their insurance, and suspected they had been ripped off, but weren't certain. Some had seen a TV program about viatical settlements, but didn't know beans about the process, the tax implications, or anything else.

The months passed. I was helping more and more people, but only those in Orange county, and only people who had AIDS. What about patients with other fatal diseases? This problem was replicated a hundred-fold throughout the state, a thousand-fold throughout the nation. Thousands of desperately ill people needed to be informed. Yet, at that point, only four advocates for the terminally ill were knowledgeable — David Peterson, Per Larson, Tom McCormack, and I. It was urgent to get the word out.

And, here it is: *Cash for the Final Days!*

TABLE OF CONTENTS

Preface
Foreword by *Ralph Nader*
Introduction..1

CHAPTER 1
Overview of Viatical Settlements........................3
Types of insurance • Types of illnesses • Mandated minimums • Accelerated Death Benefits • Partial sales • Premiums • Policy loans • The auction • Questions to ask

CHAPTER 2
The Viatical Providers..33
Funding firms • Brokers • Switch hitters • Multiple applications • Cash flow •

CHAPTER 3
All About Brokers...45
Their services • Their fees • Disclosure • Questions to ask • Being your own broker

CHAPTER 4
The Viatical Process...55
Application forms • Underwriting • Mental competency • The offer • Transfer • Escrow • Pay day • Cancellation

CHAPTER 5
Licensing: Bane or Boon?....................................71
"The Grim Reaper" and other hoary tales • Price restrictions • Disclosure rules • Medical confidentiality • Insurance agents and viatical settlements •

CHAPTER 6
Grateful for AIDS: The Brian Pardo Story.............89
The risks of dealing with Life Partners

CHAPTER 7
Your Life Insurance...123
Trouble-shooting • SGLI • VGLI • FEGLI •
Getting insurance after diagnosis

CHAPTER 8
Tax Tips..139
Non-relative dependents • Adult disabled children •
Earned income credit • Getting penalties waived •
Cashing out IRAs • Other QRT • Estate planning •
Special needs trusts • Selecting an attorney

CHAPTER 9
Look Before You Leap......................................163
Alternatives to viatication • Commercial loans •
Viatical loans • Reverse mortgages •
Discrimination • Viatical Checklist

Afterword by *Robert Hunter*............................177
Appendix I Viatical Providers.........................183
Appendix II Universal Application..................191
Appendix III Authorizations...........................194
Glossary...197
Index..201

INTRODUCTION: WHO IS THIS BOOK FOR?

Scenario 1: You are thirty years old. You've been treated for cancer (or ALS, or heart disease). Your health insurance has maxed out, and you've been told you have six months to live. While at the doctor's office, you flip through a magazine and see an advertisement about selling your life insurance for cash. You have a life insurance policy, one your parents bought years ago. Should you sell it?

Scenario 2: You are the parent who bought that life insurance twenty years ago. You've heard of scams in the viatical settlement industry. How do you help your child?

Scenario 3: Your partner has AIDS. Collection services are phoning; you're about to lose your home. You have one asset: your partner's life insurance. Should you sell?

Scenario 4: You are a social worker, an attorney, or a tax specialist. A terminally ill client asks advice about viatical settlements. What do you say?

* * *

George was the first client who asked my help selling his life insurance. He had a six month life expectancy, George told me, and was forced to sell precious antiques in order to keep his home. Days after our initial phone conversation he was gone.

This was a poignant introduction to the devastating need for cash for the final days. And it stayed with me, as I learned about the new industry that made it possible for terminally ill people to sell their life insurance. The more I learned, the more excited I became — despite knowing the dark side of the viatical industry. But once I knew the dark side, what began as a practical information book became a consumer advocacy book.

This book is an expose — of high-pressure tactics, of illegal viatical firms operating under the nose of regulators. Also exposed are traps you might fall into with so-called "legal" firms — confidentiality rights you might sign away, cancellation rights you might sacrifice.

Throughout the text you'll be reminded to deal only with viatical providers who are willing to submit to state regulation. This advice applies even if you live in a state that has no viatical law: use the list of providers approved to do business in California and/or New York.

Licensing is the first line of defense, but licensing is no guarantee of safety. Not all wolves in sheep's clothing operate illegally. A few have applied for licenses.

This book will give you tools to protect yourself. Step-by-step directions will show you how to choose a viatical provider; how to speed the application process; how to receive the most money. You'll learn what to expect — from start to finish — before you start.

* * *

If you're not terminally ill, it may surprise you to find all readers addressed as if each one of us were faced with this problem. This is intentional. This is a subject that should be taken personally. We need to step into the shoes of loved ones or clients and say, in e ffect, "This is what I would do, given the same set of circumstances."

CHAPTER 1

Overview of Viatical Settlements

Most people know little about viatical settlements — even after selling their life insurance. This chapter will give you the basic tools to take control, and help you get the largest possible settlement.

What is a viatical settlement?

The California Department of Insurance defines a viatical settlement as a contract by which a cash payment is made to a terminally ill person. This cash payment is given in exchange for the death benefits of that person's life insurance policy.

What this means is that a person who is terminally ill can sell his life insurance policy for cash.

The name of this new industry is derived from a Latin word, *viaticum* (vie-AT-uh-kum). A viaticum is an allowance for traveling expenses, or final expenses. Thus, the process of selling a life insurance policy is known as *viaticating* the policy. And the person who sells the policy is the *viator*.

What happens if I sell my life insurance?

In most situations the seller (viator) transfers all ownership rights to the buyer. This transfer is called *Absolute Assignment.* The process is no more complicated than signing a form, which is sent to the insurance company. When the transfer is made by the insurer, notice is sent to you and the buyer. When the buyer (the viatical provider) receives this notice, the funds are forwarded to you or your bank.

What ownership rights do I give up?

The most important ownership right is the right to name a beneficiary. Other ownership rights include:

- The right to take out cash values from a whole life policy.
- The right to pledge the policy as collateral.
- The right to assign the policy to another party, either for a designated period of time or permanently.

Sometimes ownership rights include the guaranteed right to increase the death benefit — without proof of health. If your policy includes this Guaranteed Insurability Option, you should get a larger viatical settlement. (See Chapters 3 and 7.)

What types of policies are purchased for viatical settlements?

Nearly every type of life insurance. You're selling death benefits, not cash values.

How can I tell if my policy qualifies?

Any life insurance policy will be considered if:

- It was issued by a financially strong insurer
- It has been in force for at least 2 years
- It is assignable (you have the right to transfer ownership and/or beneficiary rights)
- It has a level death benefit

The most important requirement is that the policy has been in force for at least two years. Other than the two-year incontestability period, there are exceptions to nearly every rule, including the "level death benefit" rule. These days, some viatical providers will buy policies with decreasing face amounts.

> Term insurance
> is as valuable as whole life.

Can I sell the policy if I'm the insured but not the owner?

Viatical providers prefer to own the policies in which they invest. Ownership assures that the policy won't *lapse*, since premium notices will come to them.[1] It also assures that you can't change the beneficiary after you spend the viaticum.

If your policy is owned by a family member, close friend, or business partner, it's usually a simple matter to have ownership transferred (converted). If the policy is owned by a life insurance trust, the trustee can sell the policy and receive the proceeds.

When problems occur, they're usually with employee group or association group. In these situations you have a certificate — not a policy. The policy (master contract) is owned by the employer or association.[2] It's best if ownership is converted to you before you attempt to sell the death benefit.

What if an employer is policy owner and refuses?

"Tough Luck." Not really — although this is what I would have said a year ago. In the past few years there have been a series of changes that favor sellers. The reason: the Law of Supply and Demand. There's a ton of money out there and too few policies for sale. This makes it a Seller's Market.

If your employer refuses to transfer ownership, some viatical providers will buy only the *beneficiary rights*. Since buyers can't take ownership, they protect their investment by being named irrevocable beneficiary.

> If ownership can't be transferred, some viatical providers will buy beneficiary rights.

How are group policies converted?

First, the insurer must send you written notice of your right to convert. Included with this notice are the conversion papers. To accept the offer, sign the conversion form and return it, enclosing a check for the first premium.

The good news is that you will be issued a standard *whole life* policy — without *evidence of insurability*. But there is a downside: The cost will be far greater than the employee group term it replaces. You may have to borrow funds to keep the conversion policy in force until you are ready to sell it or receive the insurer's *Accelerated Death Benefits*. (See below for an explanation of Accelerated Death Benefits.)

More bad news: Conversion may trigger a reduction in death benefits — possibly as low as $2,000. This is fairly common when someone's group insurance participation is less than five years. This is exactly what happened to Tom.

Tom's association policy had a face value of $250,000. When illness forced him to close his business, Tom planned to sell the policy, and use the proceeds for living expenses. That was when he learned that conversion would cause the death benefit to drop to $10,000.

> The option to convert may not be available, if you worked for a firm with less than twenty employees.

Can I sell my group term insurance before I stop working?

You could, but viatical settlements for these policies are usually discounted 5 to 7 percent below an individually owned one.[3]

Also, it may result in your employer finding out about your health problem. Before taking action, give it careful consideration: Will such disclosure lead to unbearable work conditions? (See Chapter 9 for a discussion of employment discrimination.)

How do I know if I qualify for a viatical settlement?

Anyone can qualify if they are insured, if they have been diagnosed as terminally ill, and if their life expectancy falls within the range accepted by viatical funding firms.

This range varies from six months to two years, but some viatical providers go out as far as sixty months (five years). To find the firms that match your situation, see the Appendix.

What terminal illnesses are eligible?

The illnesses most commonly accepted are AIDS; cancer; diseases of the heart, lung, or liver; hemophilia; and ALS (Lou Gehrig's disease). One funding firm that accepts heart disease does so only when it is complicated by pulmonary disease. One firm accepts leukemia; and one deals exclusively with AIDS patients.[4]

How much money will I get?

All licensed viatical providers use the same criteria, yet settlement offers may vary as much as 25 to 31 percent.[5] In one such situation, Charles had offers as low as 30 percent of face value, and as high as 70 percent. In another situation, Nick turned down an offer of 25 percent, then reapplied — this time to six additional funding firms — and sold his policy for 52 percent.

Why do offers vary so widely?

Discounts are based on a number of factors (as described in Chapter 4, *The Viatical Process*). But there is a key reason that funding firms and brokers don't tell you: cash flow. The cash position of funding firms is not steady. One day they are flush, the next day they are poor, and the next day flush again. For this reason, some won't make any offer while others who make a low offer may raise it greatly the following week.

This is one of the reasons why you should apply to several funding firms. It's also a key reason to exercise patience. Don't be tempted to leap at the first offer. Wait until all bids are in, then give the firms a chance for a second go-round. After the second go-round, if offers still seem too low, you shouldn't sell at this time.

How can I tell when an offer is too low?

A low-ball offer is one that is far removed from the guideline minimum amounts recommended by the National Association of Insurance Commissioners (NAIC). Thirty percent offers, for example: Hogwash.

What are the NAIC minimums?

The NAIC model act recommends the following minimums:

Life expectancy of Insured		% of face value paid to Viator
1 - 6 months	=	80%
6 - 12	=	70%
12 - 18	=	65%
18 - 36 months	=	60%
Beyond 36 months	=	50%

These minimums may be reduced 5 to 7 percent for group insurance. They also may be reduced up to five percent if the insurer is not deemed financially strong.[6]

Bear in mind, while the NAIC model act is not law, state laws have been designed from it. How this works in the real world can be seen from figures collected by California's Department of Insurance (DOI).

What are the California payouts?

The following figures are based on the DOI's review of the records, and are considered to be average minimums:[7]

Discount Rates (Minimum Averages)

Life expectancy of Insured		% of face value paid to Viator
3 months	=	90%
6 months	=	80%
12 months	=	70%
24 months	=	60%

What if your life expectancy is longer than 24 months? Despite an increasing number of people applying for viaticum at earlier stages of illness, California's DOI has yet to update these regulations.

This means that you must be very careful. Don't get discouraged if you only get low-ball offers. Viatical settlements aren't the only way to exchange death benefits for cash. See *Accelerated Death Benefits* (below), and Chapter 9.

Is it possible to sell a portion of my insurance?

Sell only what you must for now. Or sell one part and keep some benefits for an irrevocable beneficiary. You can do this, but it isn't easy. Many funding firms want full control. Those who buy partial benefits want to purchase at least $25,000.

> One of the least known alternatives to selling your life insurance is the option to sell only the portion that gives you the funds you need now.

What about small policies?

Amounts as small as $10,000 *can* be sold. Generally, providers who accept small policies do so on a "case-by-case" basis — which may mean,"when it's been a slow week".

If you have difficulty finding a buyer, use a broker who markets to private investment groups. But before you take this step, consider the best alternative to viatical settlements — *Accelerated Death Benefits*.

What are Accelerated Death Benefits?

Accelerated Death Benefits is a "rider" (an add-on) to cash value or term life insurance. Riders usually add or subtract from a standard policy. Riders that are added at the insured's option increase the benefits (such as the disability waiver of premium). Riders added by the insurer may subtract benefits (such as a health insurance rider that excludes coverage for an injured knee).

Accelerated Death Benefits is a rider that neither adds nor subtracts. Instead, it changes the way death benefits are paid. The ADB rider allows a terminally ill insured to receive a portion or all the death benefits that traditionally were paid to beneficiaries.

Accelerated Death Benefits (ADB) didn't exist until 1990. Today more than 3 million insureds are covered by this rider, with more insurers adding it to policies every month. Yet many insurance agents never heard of it.[8] This means that you may have to call your insurer directly, to find out if the rider is available for your policy.

If you phone the Home Office, you may find your insurer calls this rider by a different name. Variations include: Accelerated Benefits Option, Benefit Advance Endorsement, and Living Benefits.

What does the ADB cost?

Most insurers add the rider at no cost, but charge a small administrative fee if you exercise the rider. This fee may be:

- interest lost by paying out funds prior to death, or
- a percentage of the amount withdrawn — generally 3 or 4 four percent, or
- a flat rate (such as $250 or $300).

How much does the ADB pay?

The amount varies not only by insurer but sometimes by the policy issued by a particular insurer. Typical payments range from 50 to 100 percent of the death benefit. But many insurers also include a dollar cap, which may reduce the actual payout.

For example, Lincoln National offers an ADB rider that pays up to 50 percent of the death benefit — to a maximum of $250,000. New England Mutual pays 100 percent, but has the same dollar cap — $250,000.

The best paying ADB riders are from Metropolitan Life, with 90 percent and no dollar cap, and Prudential, with 100 percent and no dollar cap. However, these percentages may not be representative of all policies issued by these insurers.

Perhaps the worst ADB rider is one issued by State Farm, a commercial carrier whose primary business is property/casualty insurance (e.g., car, home, boat). State Farm arranges payment of the ADB through a bank loan. The advantage to a loan is that funds are tax free. But this loan has disadvantages.

Although it pays 60 percent of face value, if the viator lives, he is faced with a balloon note for principal and interest within 24 months.

> One client commented, "It's almost two years. I'm still alive, but I used up the money. What are they going to do? Sue me? Put me in jail?"

Then there are insurers who have different Accelerated Death Benefit riders for different policies. On a term policy issued by North American Life and Health, the "Benefit Advance Endorsement" pays 25 percent of the death benefit — to a maximum of $100,000. The same insurer has a Universal Life policy with an "Accelerated Benefit Endorsement" which also pays 25 percent — but the cap is $50,000.

Is there a down-side to the ADB?

Yes: diagnosis and life expectancy. Some insurers pay the ADB only if the rider was on your policy *before* diagnosis. And at least one insurer, New England Mutual, refuses to add it to existing insurance. But the greatest obstacle is life expectancy.

Many insurers require a life expectancy of six months or less before an insured can exercise the ADB rider. Others go out to nine months, a few go out to one year, and one or two go out as far as two years.[9]

This means that if your life expectancy is greater than your insurer's requirements, you're out of luck. Another problem: Some riders pay monthly installments, but you may need a lump sum. If any of these situations fit you, see Chapter 9.

How can I find out if my policy includes the ADB?

The rider is available with most recently-issued policies from major insurers. If your policy was issued within the last three years, the ADB rider may be listed on page one, with a description tucked into the back pages of your policy.

If your policy doesn't have the rider but your insurer allows you to add it, do so as soon as you are past the two year incontestability period. Adding the rider requires a phone call to your insurer. Use the Home Office toll free number. (If you don't have the number, ask the Information Operator: 800-555-1212). Have your policy number and social security number handy. Ask for client services. If client services never heard of Accelerated Death Benefits, ask for a supervisor.

Isn't it simpler to ask a viatical provider?

It's always easier to let someone else do the work. Before you turn this task over to a provider, consider their priorities. Viatical providers make no money unless they buy life insurance policies. Nor do they get paid for the time it takes to research this for you. Do you really want to trust them to tell you whether your insurer offers ADB?

Most viators who sold their policies in previous years never heard of Accelerated Death Benefits. And some viatical providers admit that they never inquire about it. They are content to let their brochures do the talking.

> Some viatical providers will tell you that the ADB takes much longer to get than a viatical settlement. False! It's faster!

As bleak as this may seem, a few brokers do ask viators about Accelerated Death Benefits. In one situation, the broker did all the work: contacted the insurer, and helped the client with the paperwork to apply for payment.

Is the ADB available with all types of insurance?

It's most common with cash value policies, but an increasing number of insurers now offer it with individual term, and some have begun to offer it with group insurance.

Which is better: ADB or a viaticum?

If your needs and the insurer's requirements dovetail, the ADB is a better choice. Here's why:

- Viatical settlements are paid only to terminally ill people, whereas ADB may also be used for extraordinary medical expenses, such as organ transplant, continuous life support, or long-term care.

- Viatical settlements have steep discounts, whereas the ADB rider pays dollar for dollar (less a modest administrative fee).

- ADB arrives weeks faster than a viatical settlement.

- With ADB, it's easy to get a cash payment and also leave a portion of insurance benefits for a beneficiary.

Is it possible to do a partial sale, and then apply for ADB?

Yes, but you must maintain ownership so that you can apply for Accelerated Death Benefits later on. The problem is, most viatical providers won't allow you to maintain ownership. They fear you might change the beneficiary and leave them in the lurch.

Those who might work with you on a partial sale are likely to be the same funding firms that allow insureds to keep an irrevocable beneficiary. (See the grid in the Appendix.)

The easiest way to sell partial benefits is to ask your insurer to split a large policy into smaller ones. A policy with a face amount of $50,000 could be split into two $25,000's. One policy could be viaticated and the other, at a later date, used for the ADB.

Isn't it simpler to "cash out" my insurance?

Cashing out is possible only with whole life policies, since term insurance has no cash values.[10] Yes, it *is* simpler. The problem is that you must "surrender" (give up) the policy. This means that you sign a *Surrender Form* and return it — along with the policy — to the insurer. In exchange, the insurer pays you the *net cash surrender value*. This is the sum of all savings in the policy; plus accumulated dividends (if any); plus interest on dividends (if any); less any loans and loan interest; and/or early surrender fees.

> Cashing out is simpler, but you're likely to get more money with Accelerated Death Benefits or a viatical settlement.

The problem with cashing out is that you won't have any insurance. If you choose an alternative, you might get the same amount of cash and still be insured. (See Chapter 9.)

What happens to premium payments when I sell my policy?

The new owner inherits that obligation — but there's a catch. An amount equal to premiums that will fall due for your life expectancy is subtracted from the viatical settlement. Actually, the amount subtracted is equal to *double* your life expectancy.

Premiums should be subtracted before an offer is made. In other words, settlement offers should be bottom-line offers: *net* of all expenses.

In the best-of-all possible worlds, your policy includes a

disability waiver of premium. The waiver "excuses" future premium payments, and continues after the sale — resulting in a larger viatical settlement.

What happens to policy loans?

There are two issues here: policy loans and loan interest. Policy loans reduce the death benefit, and that means a smaller viaticum. And loan *interest* continues after the sale (the waiver of premium doesn't apply to loan interest).

Once again, buyers inherit the obligation to pay annual loan interest, but in reality: you pay. Once again, buyers deduct an amount from the settlement equal to the cost of loan interest — for twice your life expectancy.

> Most viatical providers subtract from the settlement an amount equal to the cost of premiums and loan interest — for a period double that of your life expectancy.

How can I select the best viatical provider?

- Start with the list of providers eligible to do business in California and/or New York. Use these lists even if you live in a state that has its own viatical regulation. And if your state has no viatical regulation, it's even more important to use firms licensed by California and/or New York. The reason: These states have strict rules governing viatical contracts — rules designed to protect you. (Details about licensing can be found in Chapter 5.)

Don't consider any company that hasn't applied for a viatical license. While licensing laws have limited ability to protect you, the true value of licensing may be far more subtle. According to financial planner David Peterson, "Willingness to make a public filing of information may, at least, indicate a level of seriousness and good intentions."[11]

That said, let's return to the process of selecting viatical providers:

- When you phone for application materials, pepper them with questions.
- Apply to at least three providers (preferably six!) or three and a broker, if you decide to use a broker.
- Run an auction.

What is meant by "run an auction"?

Picture this: Three firms spend time and money underwriting your application. The offers come in. Company A looks good; Company B looks better; Company C is tops.

Now you start the auction: "Sorry, Company A/B. I've been offered 10 percent more by Company C." Companies A and B may ask to see the higher offers, to assure that they are valid. This is why you insist on written offers.

This auction (or bidding war) can be run between two brokers, a handful of funding firms, or broker versus funding firms.

Why will they up their bids?

It's a Seller's Market. Before the viatical industry came into being, life insurance was just a piece of paper. Then there were one, two, three funding firms; sellers had to take what they could get. Now there are several dozen such firms, and a ton of money sitting idle, waiting for policies to buy.

Secondly, viatical providers spend a chunk of money getting to the point where they make an offer. If you turn them down, they won't recover their administrative expenses.

Also, the funding firm might get a sudden infusion of cash. Then they could offer more.[12]

What kinds of questions should I ask viatical providers?

Depending on your situation, check:

- **Policy size** requirements. Some viatical firms will not buy very large policies. Either their funds are limited, or they consider these amounts too risky. Some will not consider small policies (below a certain dollar amount).

- **Partial sale**, if you want to keep a portion of benefits, whether for an irrevocable beneficiary or to sell at a later time. Some funding firms will not consider partial sales.

- **Life expectancy.** Does your life expectancy fit their requirements?

- **Expenses.** There should be none. Don't pay a fee for application, for acquiring your medical records, for prescriptions, credit cards, or any other services. Do not pay a fee for "due diligence."

- **Confidentiality.** Brokers must share your medical history when they shop your policy, but you have a right to know who will have access to confidential information. Will it go to funding companies? Pension managers? Individual investors?

- **Escrow.** Will the escrow company notify you when funds are deposited in your name?

- **Full disclosure** of:

— all offers (if using a broker).

— all referral fees. You are entitled to know if a referral by your physician, social case-worker, financial planner, lawyer, or other advisor was influenced by a fee.

New York law requires disclosure of fees, but only one funding firm (Legacy Benefits) and one broker (Life Today) voluntarily provide this information to all viators, regardless of where they live. This disclosure is part of their sales agreements.

- **Resale.** Do providers intend to hold your policy until maturity, or will they resell it? Some funding companies resell policies in a "secondary market." They may get a higher price than you were paid; or perhaps they were forced to sell in order to get funds to buy a policy with a shorter pay off than yours.

Most of these questions apply to both types of viatical providers — funding firms or brokers. Ask for written answers to all questions to be enclosed with application materials. If they don't comply, you may add it to the contract yourself — and request that additions be initialized by a principal and a copy returned to you.

Why should I apply to several funding firms?

California's DOI (Department of Insurance) recommends applying to three funding sources. Per Larson and David Peterson, financial advisors who have assisted hundreds of terminally ill, recommend no less than five providers. David Peterson is particularly emphatic about six — despite his awareness that it takes between 8 and 15 hours of work for so many applications.

Here's why six applications are essential. Frequently one provider doesn't respond at all. A second may phone to explain why they won't make an offer. A third may make an offer that is painfully low-ball.

Joe's situation is a perfect example. He applied to three firms directly and three through a broker. One funding firm never responded. Another refused to bid (through the broker), claiming that Joe's life expectancy was too far out to pin down. Of the four remaining, Joe eventually accepted an offer of 58%. But what if he had applied to only one provider, as so many viators do? And if that one never responded?

Sure it's a headache to do that paperwork. Make it worth your while. Tell the providers you're applying to others. If they expect competition, they'll be prepared to negotiate.

You can make your task easier by using the Universal Application and Authorizations in the Appendix. Make copies, or put the disk on your computer and fill in the names of each viatical provider. See the order form on the last page.

Or, enlist a broker to do much of the work for you.

What can a broker do for me?

A good broker can save you time, save you work, relieve you of the stress of negotiating, find buyers for problem insurance, and very possibly get you higher bids than you could get on your own.

But brokers don't always have the best deals. Some may not market your insurance to more than two funding firms. Some may not bring you the highest offer. Don't place all your trust in one broker. Give them competition. (For details about working with a broker, see Chapter 3.)

In order to verify offers from the broker, you must see them. Insist on *written* offers. No less important: before signing a contract with a broker, insist that the broker agree — in writing — to full disclosure of referral fees.

New York prohibits payment of finder's fees to anyone involved in the medical, legal, or financial care of viators, and requires full disclosure of all other referral fees. Although you may live outside New York, this doesn't prevent you from requiring disclosure for yourself.

Bottom line: If you are fully informed and decide to use a broker, a good broker may be worth his/her weight in gold.

> Brokers are savvy enough to know that a smaller commission is better than ZILCH!

How do broker commissions influence the offers?

By law, broker fees are not supposed to come out of your settlement. This means that purchase offers must be *net* of all expenses. You should get exactly what's offered, nothing less.

But that's the end result. Behind the scenes, brokers have fee agreements with various funding firms. One fee agreement may pay them 6 or 7 percent. Another may pay only 4 percent.

These fees have nothing to do with what you receive. This is 6 percent of the policy's death benefit!

Since broker's income doesn't depend on getting you the best deal, they have no financial incentive to haggle on your behalf. Whether you get 30 percent or 70 percent, they get the same fee.

> If you use a broker to sell a policy with a face value of $100,000, this is what may occur:
>
> • Company A offers you 80% ($80,000)
> and pays a broker 4% ($ 4,000)
>
> • Company B offers you 70% ($70,000)
> and pays a broker 6% ($ 6,000)
>
> If you were the broker, which would you choose?

adapted from "Was that Buy Low, Sell High, Or...?" Per Larson, Positively Aware, July/Aug. 1995.

This is why some brokers will bring you one — just one single offer. The one that represents the highest broker fee.

The remedy: Never use only one broker.

How long does the process take?

From the time you submit the applications until you have the cash: four to six weeks.[13] However, if your policy is complicated or flawed, the entire process may take as long as four months. To check whether your insurance policy has these problems, see Chapter 7.

Why does it take so long?

Details of The Viatical Process are in Chapter 4.

Won't multiple applications slow the process?

That's what viatical providers will tell you. Is it any wonder they don't want you to solicit bids from their competitors? The fact is: to some degree, they're right. Multiple applications can slow the process.

Imagine this: a half dozen requests for medical records hit your doctor's office. Imagine how crazy this makes the office staff! Imagine the same when a half dozen requests hit the insurance company.

Of course, it will take longer.

But is your haste so great that you are willing to give up another 10 percent? 25 percent? Perhaps 50 percent? Or are you willing to wait another two weeks in order to get several thousand dollars more?

If you're still not sure, think about Jerry. He refused an offer of 30 percent from the one company to which he applied on his own. Then he took my advice. He applied to five others — three on direct application and two through a broker. This meant another wait of six weeks. But when he sold his policy, he was paid $57,400 more than the initial offer.[14]

Will my employer be contacted?

There's no reason to do so, if your insurance is privately owned. But contacting your employer may be unavoidable, if your insurance is Group Life, and hasn't been converted to your ownership. If contact must be made with your employer, it's done only with your permission and written authorization.

What if I change my mind about selling?

No problem — at any time before you receive the settlement. One phone call from you and the process comes to a screeching halt. Follow up with a letter that formally cancels the tentative agreement.

Note that once your mattress bulges with cash, you have 15 days to rescind (cancel) without penalty. (Some states have a grace period of 30 days.)

In the event you may cancel, take a magnifying glass to the fine print in your agreement. You'll find some funding firms have laid land mines for the unwary who dare to rescind. (For details, see Chapter 4.)

How are viatical providers informed when an insured dies?

They don't refer to it as an insured dying. They say, "*The policy matured*."

Most funding sources do their own tracking of viators after the sale, but a few brokers do it for them — in order to earn additional fees. The most popular method is to give viators self-addressed post cards, with instructions to return one each month. These post cards ask you to confirm your address and doctor, or to supply revised information.

Some providers don't contact you directly. Instead, they ask for names of close friends or relatives. Funding firm Legacy Benefits contacts one person on your list every three months, so that no one is bothered more than once a year. Not only have they never had anyone object, a few contacts took the initiative to inform them when the viator passed away.

> "One broker offers the delightful service of client follow-up. For another 1 to 2 percent, this broker follows the person to the death — and reports to the funding firm."
> — Per Larson

Alternately, some funding firms contact your doctor — putting to further use your Medical Authorization.

Page & Associates has an unique method. They offer additional services at no cost. This program, Better Benefits for Life, provides viators with a national case counselor phone line twenty-four hours a day, serviced by a licensed RN. They also provide a discount service for prescription drugs, medical equipment and supplies, and a legal phone line.

Is the viatical settlement taxable?

Yes and no. Neither viatical settlements nor Accelerated Death Benefits are taxed at the state level by California or New York. And the news gets better. It's expected that these funds will become tax free on the federal level, when the budget is passed.[15]

However, if the bill to make these benefits tax free becomes law, it will affect only those people whose life expectancies are two years or less. Beyond two years, these payments will continue to be taxable.

How is the tax calculated?

Viatical settlements and Accelerated Death Benefits are taxed as ordinary income. To learn how to calculate the taxable portion — the gain — as well as how to save tax dollars, see Chapter 8.

Will my Social Security or other public assistance be reduced or terminated?

Not under present law. Neither Social Security Disability (SSDI) nor Medicare will be reduced or discontinued. The right to these benefits is based on disability.

However, "means-based" (also called "needs-based") benefits are likely to be affected. This includes Supplemental Security Income (SSI), food stamps, welfare, Medicaid and its state-named derivatives (e.g., Medi-Cal or Cal-Optima in California).

How are means-based benefits affected?

In order to qualify for means-based benefits, financial need must be shown. You won't have this need in the month that you receive a lump sum cash payment for your life insurance. For that month, means-based benefits will be forfeited. And for the time that any of these funds remain, they are assets and will disqualify you for public assistance.

Of course you can reapply, once the viatical settlement is depleted. And the money will disappear quickly, if you pay medical costs out of pocket. Instead of putting yourself through the hassle a second time, sell your insurance *before* government benefits are needed.

How do government agencies find out about the viaticum?

Not from viatical firms. Nor from insurers (other than government insurance). There is no requirement for viatical firms or insurers to report these sums, or to send out 1099s (although this could change at any time).

Unless requirements change, the only way that government agencies will find out is from you. If you are asked about your current financial status and don't disclose these funds, and if you continue to accept means-based government benefits, you could be liable for welfare fraud.

If I sell one policy now and a second one next year, should I use the same viatical provider?

Viatical providers will tell you, "Yes, because it's faster than starting all over again." Don't buy that line. If your health is worse next time round, the provider may offer you the same percentage as before — when you should get more. If your health improves, however, you can bet they'll find out — and adjust the settlement offer downward.

There is yet another reason for shopping the marketplace. Remember that ole bugaboo, Cash Flow? You may have made your request at a time when the funding firm's coffers were empty. Without competing offers, how will you know whether this is a low-ball offer?

How do I get started?

- First, get professional advice about your financial and tax situation.

• Next, share this book with your advisors. Most professional advisors know little or nothing about viatical settlements — but may not admit this to your face. Once they have this information, you can ask their advice about viatical settlements.

• Then, check with your insurer about Accelerated Death Benefits, or splitting your policy, or both.

• If you decide to apply for a viatical settlement, line up emotional support — family and friends.

* * *

END NOTES

1. This is true of term or whole life insurance, but not necessarily so with Universal or Variable Life policies.

2. Associations include alumni groups, professional groups, sports groups.

3. According to David Peterson, who founded Affording Care, the New York non-profit organization that provides educational services and benefit information to the terminally ill.

4. American Life Resources used to deal exclusively with people with AIDS, while its sibling, Living Benefits, dealt exclusively with all other terminal illness but AIDS. In 1996 both firms, which are funded by National Capital Benefits Corporation, broadened their scope to all terminal illnesses.

5. Based primarily on records of more than 200 viators assisted by Per Larson, a New York-based financial advisor and advocate.

6. Public libraries usually have copies of A.M. Best, and other independent rating services (Moody's, and Standard & Poor's).

7. From an informational memo provided to consumers by California's DOI. For a copy, phone 1-800-927-HELP. Out of state, phone 1-213-897-8921.

8. The National Insurance Consumer Helpline (800-942-4242) is a consumer information telephone service sponsored by insurance industry trade associations.

9. North American Life & Health has term policies in which ADB is paid when life expectancy is one year. The same insurer goes out to two years on Universal Life policies.

10. Whole life policies are known as cash value policies, ordinary life, or permanent insurance. Cash value policies include flexible premium Universal Life; and flexible premium Variable Life.

11. From David Peterson's unpublished manuscript, Process of Viatication, Draft V, November 10, 1994.

12. This point was stressed repeatedly by David Peterson.

13. Based on phone interviews with viatical providers, David Peterson, Per Larson, and Thomas McCormack — the linchpins of financial planning for the terminally ill — and firsthand accounts reported by clients of AIDS Services Foundation.

14. Per Larson has a name for people who try to make their own sale, then ask for help: "refugees."

15. The Wall St. Journal (12/18/95) reported that lobbying and donations by the insurance industry resulted in tax incentives for consumers, including the bill to make accelerated death benefits tax free — whether paid by an insurer or a viatical provider.

CHAPTER 2

The Viatical Providers

Everyone in this new industry is a pioneer. Exactly who are these viatical providers? Can they be trusted? Is there a blueprint for choosing a good company?

Who are the viatical providers?

At this writing, there are more than fifty viatical providers in the nation. Most are licensed (or have applied for licenses) in California and New York — the two states with the greatest population of potential viators. These states also have the most stringent licensing requirements. For these reasons, people who wish to sell their life insurance should deal exclusively with companies on the California and/or New York Insurance Departments' lists. This is especially true, if you live in a state that has not enacted viatical regulation.

Not all viatical providers are alike. In fact, there are two distinct types — funding firms and brokers — as well as a third category, switch-hitters.

What are "funding firms"?

They are the Daddy Warbucks of the industry, direct buyers who self fund their purchases.[1] With the exception of ViatiCare, which doesn't accept brokered applications, you may sell directly to a funding firm, or you may sell to them through a broker.

Most funding firms buy and hold life insurance policies as part of their investment portfolios, but some re-sell them in "the secondary market."

> "We set the price for the market because we're the ones with the ready money. If we make an offer today and it's accepted, we can get funds tomorrow."
> — John Warburton (Life Entitlements)

Since funding firms assume all the risks, they make the rules: what diseases to accept, what life expectancies to accept, and what types of insurance to accept. Three years ago, most funding firms didn't accept group insurance. Now they do. One year ago, most viatical providers put all their financial energies into marketing to AIDS patients. Now they're broadening their scope to other fatal diseases.

At this writing, twenty-one funding firms are licensed to

solicit viatical contracts in California, and another nine are permitted to do so while their licenses are pending.[2]

How are viatical brokers different from funding firms?

Brokers are like realtors: go-betweens who help you sell your insurance policy. Since brokers are intimately involved in the viatical process, have access to your medical records, and can influence the amount of settlement, they are subject to the same viatical regulations as funding firms.

> "Brokers don't make the rules.
> Funding firms make the rules.
> We have to learn them, and play their game."
> — Scott Wilbanks, broker

Who are the switch-hitters?

These are viatical providers who operate in both capacities — as funding sources and brokers. In early 1995 there were a handful of switch-hitters. Now the only funding firm that admits to routinely acting as a switch-hitter is Life Today. Life Today is listed with the California DOI as a funding source, but its primary function is broker — through Life Financial Services (its brokerage arm).

According to Rick Perry, president of both companies, Life Financial Services seeks funding for insurance policies not accepted for purchase by Life Today. To get the best price for viators, Perry will shop an applicant to as many as eight funding firms.

Where did the other switch-hitters go? The Appendix lists several firms that existed but went out of business in the past year. Then there are funding firms like Access, which flipped into a brokerage, and brokers like Page & Associates, which flipped into a funding firm. Scott Wilbanks (Wilbanks and Associates) sees this as a commonplace occurrence:

> "Viatical companies have a shorter life expectancy than the clients they work with. Every six months the industry has a very different face. Brokers switch and become funding companies, funding companies run out of funds and become brokers. Some flip-flop back and forth. This makes it very difficult to know who is still in business."

There are occasional switch-hitters — funding firms that act as broker once in a while, usually on the request of a viator. Lisa Schub (Legacy Benefits) tells the story of a woman with cancer. When Legacy Benefits were "unable to pin down her life expectancy" and rejected her, the distraught woman cried, "What am I to do?" Schub took it upon herself to phone other funding firms, and found one that would accept the woman. To expedite the process, she sent the woman's medical and insurance files to the other firm.

Paulette of Life Benefactors tells a similar story. But Life Benefactors, listed as a funding firm, acts as broker with such frequency that it has a special form for marketing policies.

Tucked into the standard application kit, this form, "Supplemental Authorization for Release of Medical and Other Information," gives Life Benefactors permission to act as a broker, and to release clients' records to any prospective buyer.

A client who wants to apply directly to funding firms (and not through a broker) will find an application to Life Benefactors is an "either-or" contract: Either we'll buy your policy, or we'll broker it.

I learned about this from Frank, who asked me to review the applications he was about to sign. His dining table was covered with tall stacks of paper, one stack for each of the six firms to which he was applying. Waving the Supplementary Authorization in the air, he said, "Do I have to read this?"

"You don't have to read it," I told him. "I will."

> Viators who sign this form "waive the provisions of California Health and Safety Code Section 199, et seq., relating to such tests or information, and the provisions of California Civil Code Section 56 (the 'Confidentiality of Medical Information Act') as they relate to any confidentiality I have in my medical records."

I didn't like this form. Moreover, no other provider asks for a complete waiver of confidentiality rights. I advised Frank not to sign. Life Benefactors' standard medical authorization was enough. I was certain that this one omission wouldn't impair his application. Not when viatical providers view the possibility of buying a life insurance policy the way starving wolves view a hen house.

As to the issue of funding firms "brokering" policies, it's not illegal, but I find it disturbing. You should know when you apply whether your confidential records will stay "in house" or be marketed broadly. And if they *are* marketed broadly, you have a right to know to whom: other funding firms? investor groups? individuals?

Where do funding firms get their money?

Most funding firms began with private money, then added a bank credit line. Here's a sampling:

Viaticus began as a small funding firm, founded by a widower after his wife died of cancer.[3] In 1994, this small company was purchased by a large national insurer, CNA. This gave Viaticus an unusually "deep pocket" which, in turn, gave them the ability to finance very large policies as well as long life expectancies — as far out as five years.

Dignity Partners combined bank money with the financial resources of three individuals — and continued to grow. In 1995, Dignity Partners repackaged $35 million worth of life insurance, which they sold to a Connecticut-based investment bank.[4] These policies represented 300 viators, mainly AIDS patients, none with life expectancies greater than three years. Before marketing the policies, Dignity Partners had them rated by Standard & Poor's. They were assigned an "A" rating.

Later that year, Dignity Partners went public and currently trade on NASDAQ as DPNR. Now they can raise capital through the stock market.

ViatiCare Financial Services was started by a PLWA (Person Living With AIDS). Adam Tillis had sold his policy a few years earlier. Five months after he applied, Tillis got his settlement:

30 cents on the dollar. This was a typical payout for those pre-regulation years, but the experience gave Tillis an idea.

His career in commercial insurance had given Tillis numerous contacts among the rich and famous. One of these contacts was Paul Moe, president of Marquee Management, a Minneapolis-based company that oversees business and legal affairs for American artists and entertainers overseas.[5] Moe and Tillis assembled a management team, enlisted initial investors, acquired a bank credit line and a Chicago-based pension fund, and created a new funding firm: ViatiCare.

These stories are typical of the funding firms on the DOI's list. But there are other funding firms, ones that operate "underground." They slip illegally past the borders of states like California, buy policies for which they have no funds; go on hunting expeditions (for funds) after policies are transferred to them; and some don't pay the viators — ever. More on this in Chapters 5 and 6.

> Empty Claims:
> "We pay more than any other firms."
> "We're the oldest."
> "We're the largest."
> "We promise to make a donation
> to your favorite charity."

How can I know which companies to avoid?

Consider this a Cardinal rule: Avoid all companies that have not applied for a viatical license. At least a half dozen "underground" viatical companies operate in states like

California and New York. They claim to pay more than licensed companies, and sometimes they do — to a few viators, for public relations purposes. Usually they don't. They don't, primarily because they haven't the same credibility with banks as licensed funding firms. This leads them to raise funds from individuals. Which means that individuals become the owners of these policies.

Individual buyers tend to panic when viators outlive their life expectancies. Panic leads them to phone the viator, again and again, checking on the state of the viator's health.

Another empty claim unlicensed firms make is that they use an escrow trust (just like licensed companies). This may be true; then again, the "escrow company" may be Uncle Joe's mattress. There's no check on unlicensed companies, because there is no law governing them.

For this reason, David Peterson, founder of the New York-based nonprofit Affording Care, suggests California registration as a starting point for anyone seeking a viatical provider.

> "Registration means that the firms have supplied the state with information about the company and its principals; it does not mean that California insurance department has made any judgment about the company. Willingness to make a public filing of information may, at least, indicate a level of seriousness and good intentions."[6]

How about a company that advertises in national magazines?

Some of the least trustworthy viatical companies are vividly and expensively displayed. Some of the safer, more reputable ones rarely advertise.

What about a firm whose president was on TV, or who spoke at a local seminar?

There's a payoff for being dramatic, flamboyant, or controversial: lots of free publicity.

How about endorsement by a nonprofit organization?

Endorsement by a nonprofit is just as valid as a car or toothpaste endorsement by your favorite screen star.

What about a firm headed by a PLWA?

The individual whose name is on the masthead is not the key. Registration is. Registration, information, and competition.

How about a company run by gays?

Per Larson warns against unquestioned trust of people who use their connection to the gay community. He described one such individual: "He positions himself as a gay advocate. But his profit margin is very substantial. It goes to support a very high life style."

Is there a blueprint for going through the viatical process?

There is now.

- Begin with the California or New York Department of Insurance (DOI) list.
- Compare the list with the grid in the Appendix. This will

help you identify which providers suit your situation.

- Get information. Ask questions when you phone for application kits. (See Chapters 1 and 3 for questions.) When you phone, watch out for empty claims.

- When you receive the application kits, and you feel overwhelmed by all the paperwork, there are three ways to simplify the chore:

(1) Fill in the easiest questionnaire (discarding the rest). Make copies to send to all firms to which you are applying. Remember, at least 3 — preferably 5 — funding firms.

(2) Or use the Universal Application in the Appendix. Copy it, and enlarge to letter size (8½" x 11"). Fill it in once. Make copies to send to all providers.

(3) Use the order form at the back of the book to send for the Universal Application kit, or a computer disk. With the exception of ViatiCare, all funding firms agreed to accept this Universal forms — just as they accept forms designed by individual brokers.

- If you use a provider's application, omit details about your medical history. They need only know how to contact your doctors, hospitals, clinics, etc. They'll learn what they need from your medical records. And don't worry about being persnickety. This is a Seller's Market.

- Read, then sign the authorization forms. If you use the Universal Authorizations, insert each provider's name in the appropriate place. Each provider needs an Authorization bearing its own name.

- Insist on *written* offers. This applies whether you apply through a broker or go directly to the funding firms. Add a statement to this effect to the agreement. Keep a copy of all completed forms for your records.

- Mail all applications on the same day. This gives each provider equal time to procure your records and decide on an offer.

* * *

END NOTES

1. Funding firms also are known as funding sources and capitalization firms.

2. Applicants for a viatical license are allowed to begin business 60 days after filing required documents with the Department of Insurance — unless they have been ordered not to do so.

3. Best Week, Life/Health Edition, August 8, 1994, published by A.M. Best, Inc.

4. "S.F. Investment Company Sells 'Death Notes,'" Arthur M. Louis. San Francisco Chronicle, March 4, 1995.

5. "Cash and Dignity for the Dying," Rick Nelson, Corporate Report Minnesota, September 1994. Reprint available from ViatiCare.

6. Process of Viatication, David Peterson, Draft VI, Dec. 21, 1994.

CHAPTER 3

All About Viatical Brokers

Brokers save clients time and energy, and greatly reduce the stress of the viatical process. They may even get you more money than you could get on your own. But how do you find the good ones? And what's behind their claim of free services?

Who are they?

Unlike funding firms, it doesn't take zillions of dollars to be a broker. Nor does it require any specialized knowledge. This is why brokers are such a diverse group. They come from a multitude of directions and professions, including insurance, real estate, law, nursing, or financial planning.

Some brokerages are luxury sized (a number of employees); some medium range (one or two employees); and a few are "subcompacts" (sole proprietors). Regardless of size, they operate pretty much alike, since larger brokerages will assign you to work with one individual.

Since brokers have nothing to offer but services, good service is bread and butter to them.

What services do brokers provide?

Most viators have fond memories of brokers' frequent phone calls. Clients who also applied directly to funding firms spoke about the remarkable contrast. With funding firms, it's not uncommon to hear nothing from Day of Application to Day of Offer. Worse, yet: Some viators never hear from one or more funding firms. Reputable brokers know which funding firms match your situation. They also know which funding firms are in a buying mood.

> Deborah Rhoades (Viatical Clearing House) said that new funding firms phone brokers to announce their eagerness to buy.
> This was confirmed by Carol Fiedler (Fiedler Financial): funding firms call brokers to announce when they are flush with funds.

- If you apply directly to funding firms as well as a broker, if the highest offer is from the direct application, the broker will go back to the funding sources to get a higher offer. If the broker's funding sources refuse to increase their bid, rather than lose the sale the broker is likely to cut his/her commission. This is how you may get more money when you use a broker.
- Negotiations. Brokers can do the haggling for you. But

will they? This is why you want written offers. Written offers are the only way to ensure that a broker has approached at least three funding sources.

- Do you have a policy that's difficult to place with a funding firm? Some brokers have alternative buyers: individual investors, investment groups, or pension funds.

> "I wouldn't sell to individual investors. But I have private pension groups who work exclusively with me. And they pay more than viatical firms. Why? Because with funding firms this is their business: They have to cover their overhead; they have to raise money. With pension plans the money is there; they simply have to find ways to invest."
> — Deborah Rhoades (Viatical Clearing House)

- Additionally, some brokers are competent to provide insurance advice.

What kind of insurance advice do brokers provide?

- Advice about Accelerated Death Benefits. Brokers claim they always inquire about ADB — and some do.

- Advice on timing. If you are employed, a good broker will question whether this is the best time for you to viaticate. For a discussion on timing, as well as alternatives to viatication, see Chapter 9.

- Advice on which policy to viaticate. If you have two policies, a knowledgeable broker can advise which one to sell. The reason for choosing one over the other shouldn't be solely because of a larger death benefit. To better understand features of your life insurance that relate to viatical settlements, see Chapter 7.

- Advice about maximizing your settlement. One example is this suggestion made by David Landay, the broker who heads National Viator Representatives (NVR).

> "Retain the rights to any guaranteed increase(s) in the face amount of your policy, or negotiate a fair price for their rights at the time of sale."[1]

Landay doesn't explain, but here's what he means:

Your policy may include the right to increase the death benefit by simply filling in a form — and without proof of health! This is done in one of two ways:

1. Guaranteed Insurability Option (GIO). This rider may be attached to either whole life or term insurance. It allows an insured to increase the death benefit by acting on the option date. This may be your birthday, or the policy anniversary date. Doing this may increase the premium, but we're not talking big bucks. We're talking ten cents on the dollar.

2. Increasing face amount option (also known as Level II).

This feature is common to Universal and Variable Life policies. If your policy has a level death benefit, the face amount remains the same forever. But you may choose to change from a level death benefit to an increasing amount (Level II), if the policy has substantial cash values. Level II causes the cash values to be added to the death benefit and instantly increases the face amount.

Who pays the broker?

In states with viatical regulation, what you see is what you get. In other words, purchase offers from licensed brokers are net of fees and expenses. This is the basis for brokers' claims that their services are free — they are paid by the buyer. It sounds good — until you lift the flap and peek into the tent.

This is what Per Larson found:

- All brokers have a "structural conflict of interest." Since their fees are tied to the face amount of the policy (not the amount you get), there is no motivation for them to haggle for price.

- Some brokers have fee agreements with only two funding firms. Two funding firms means these brokers don't shop a client's file.

- Since all brokers have contractual agreements with funding firms, they know in advance exactly how much they'll be paid. This is why some brokers won't bring to the table offers from funding firms that pay less than 6 percent — even if the offer means thousands more for you.

But there is another side to this. Some brokers have the exact same fee agreement with all funding firms. This levels the playing field and allows them to work on behalf of clients — without taint of influence.

Larson believes that viators get less when they use a broker, but Carole Fiedler (Fiedler Financial) said the opposite is true. As proof, she cites the following:

- Funding firms allocate a percentage of operating expenses for broker commissions.

- When a broker provides the entire document package, it spares the funding firm this expense. This, in turn, reduces staffing needs and overhead expenses for the funding firm.

Fiedler's argument is buttressed by funding firm, Dignity Partners. Dignity Partners, which doesn't advertise, depends on brokers to bring business to their door. As Alan Perper, one of the firm's founders, explained:

> "What a lot of people don't understand is that brokers incur a lot of up-front costs, but they don't get paid until a policy sells. If we incurred these expenses for every policy, regardless of whether we funded it or not, our overhead would be that much higher. This way, we don't pay expenses for policies we don't buy, and we don't pay brokers until a policy actually is funded."[2]

The result, Perper said, "Brokers not only save our company money but actually allow us to offer more money to clients."

John Warburton (Life Entitlements) agreed. "If a client came to us independently and we made an offer of 70 percent, with a broker we may give them a range of 75-80 percent, and pay the broker fee on top."

How do clients find a broker?

Several funding firms use public seminars to attract clients, but Life Today appears to be the only broker that does this.[3] Life Today, located in Texas, hires a hall or gym in the Houston area, signs on an estate planning attorney and a financial planner, and runs these seminars for community groups or hospital employees.

Instead of seminars, most large brokerages (and many funding firms) routinely pay four thousand a month for a full page ad.[4] Although little brokers also advertise, usually it's through little ads and not on a regular basis. This doesn't mean they don't get publicity. They keep a welcome mat ready for any media person who offers a public relations freebie. You can see the results for yourself: copies of these feature articles are tucked into every application kit they send out.

Unlike other brokers, Scott Wilbanks sees it as a point of pride not to advertise. Referrals serve him very well, thank you, and Wilbanks has no ambition to obtain clients beyond the Bay area — particularly since he prides himself on meeting personally with all viators.

This hoity-toity local-only attitude is not shared by other brokers. Other brokers have spasms of ecstacy when they get clients from far-flung states. Nor is this true of Wilbanks, as Sherrid discovered.[5]

> Sherrid revealed that Susan Stanfield, a supervising social worker at AIDS Foundation Houston, moonlights as a local representative of Wilbanks & Associates. "Should a caregiver be linked to an enterprise that benefits from the patient's timely death?"

"Enriching the Final Days," U.S. News & Wld. Rpt.

The fact is, most brokers rely heavily on referrals. And most viators find brokers through referral. If you're lucky, it'll work for you. But you may be running a risk — particularly if the referring party has a hand in the broker's pocket.

Pamela Sherrid, writing for U.S. News & World Report, tells of physicians who ask for "a direct commission of 1 percent of the death benefit for each client they send to a viatical firm."

There is no safe way to find a trustworthy broker unless you start with the DOI's list, ask questions when you phone, and use referrals only to short-list the ones you have checked.

> Most brokers and funding firms
> pay referral fees to COI.
> These "Centers of Influence" may be
> your doctor, your lawyer, your accountant,
> your financial planner, or your caseworker.

What questions should I ask brokers?

The following list was compiled from phone conversations and articles authored by Per Larson, and reports from my clients. When you phone, be prepared to jot down answers. If the answers satisfy you, insist that these answers be added to the broker agreement and the purchase agreement.

- What companies do you deal with?

Even if you don't live in California or New York, you want funding firms that are listed in at least one of these states (as well as your own state, if your state has regulation). License-pending companies may be as good as those who have been fully licensed.

- What commissions do these companies pay?

Since commissions vary from funding firm to funding firm, you want to know if the broker has a financial incentive to direct clients to a particular funding firm.

- Is your broker commission negotiable?

The broker may tell you this is unimportant since it is the

buyer who pays the commission, which means these services are free to viators. But the fee is negotiable. One viator was so disappointed with the offers that he was reluctant to accept any. At that point the broker sliced the fee, and the client received two thousand more.

- Will you insist on offers in writing? Will you agree to show me all of them? Be warned: Brokers don't like to do this. Most play with the deck close to their chests.

- Who is the ultimate buyer?

> "The viator should be very much aware who is the ultimate buyer. If I was a private investor I would go nuts. I would call him every day to ask: 'Are you still alive?' But *I* don't care. You know why I don't care? It's the aggregate. We have hundreds of viators. Some are still alive from when we started the business in 1991."
>
> — Meir Eliav
> (Legacy Benefits)

Can I be my own broker?

If your insurance is not complicated — yes. But if it's complicated, it's doubtful you'll be able to sell it without help.

Here's how to do-it-yourself:

- Start with the DOI's list. Compare it with the grid in the Appendix. Begin phoning.

- Send for your medical and insurance records. Make copies, and enclose one copy with each application. For details about collecting records, see Chapter 4.

- Be prepared to negotiate hard. Or enlist a friend, relative, or financial advisor do this for you.

A word of caution: Some viatical providers are fearful of client-provided documents. Lisa Schub is an administrator at Legacy Benefits, a funding firm that doesn't accept client-provided documents. Schub said, "Getting the records directly is the only way to protect the confidence of investors."

This view is buttressed by Deborah Rhoades (Viatical Clearing House). Rhoades was burned by a client who wasn't terminally ill but submitted false lab and medical records.

Despite these views, most funding firms welcome your help. So go for it.

* * *

END NOTES

1. From the marketing book authored by Landay, "Every Question You Need to Ask Before Selling Your Life Insurance Policy." The 66-page book is distributed free by National Viator Representatives (800) 932-0050.

2. From a telephone interview with Alan Perper.

3. Funding firms Dignity Partners and Neuma use community seminars as marketing tools.

4. Numerous viatical advertisements can be found in the Advocate, a Los Angeles based magazine for gay people; Coping, a magazine for cancer patients; and POZ, a magazine for people who are HIV positive.

5. U.S. News & World Report, August 25 1995.

CHAPTER 4

The Viatical Process

Why does the viatical process takes 6 to 8 weeks? How do funding firms decide on an offer? Is there a way to prevent low-ball offers? What if I change my mind?

Why does it take so long to get a settlement?

Usually it's doctors who hold things up — by not providing medical records on a timely basis. Other times it's the insurer that doesn't respond promptly. But snags could occur at nearly every stage of the viatical process.

How it begins:

When you phone for an application kit, brokers and funding firms alike will ask your diagnosis, and whether your insurance policy is personally owned or through an employer, and whether the policy is past the two year incontestability period.

These three basic questions determine if your health and insurance policy fit the firm's guidelines. Some viatical providers may ask about life expectancy. Don't worry if you don't have an answer. Most doctors are reluctant to tell their patients.

Some viatical providers may ask detailed medical questions on the phone. If they do, hang up. If they give you an estimate of the settlement offer, hang up.

"DANGER SIGNALS"
"1. Claims that ADB take longer than viatication (they're faster).
2. Hard-sell tactics.
3. Efforts to get you to sign an "exclusive" contract.
4. Estimates or offers given without records or policy information in hand.
5. Extravagant asset claims."

Viatication Guidelines, Per Larson Sept. 1994.

Since all firms use overnight couriers, application packets should arrive the following day. One funding firm has a ten page questionnaire; some use five pages; and a rare few have pared it down to one page.[1] Here's how to turn intimidating into workable:

- Skip questions that are intrusive or inappropriate. Skip questions that ask for detailed medical information: Your medical records will furnish the necessary details. If they ask about your employment but your policy is privately owned, skip that section, also.

• Add to each questionnaire the following words: "Only written Settlement Offers will be considered."

• Sign authorizations for release of medical and insurance information.

• If you apply to several funding firms, this procedure will have to be repeated for each company. If you don't skip details, you can expect to spend approximately an hour and a half for each application.

Or, you could apply through a broker (or two). This would limit your labors to one (or two) brokers' applications and authorizations, but result in 3 to 6 offers.

Or, use the questionnaire that looks easiest, and send copies to all companies. Attach a sticky note to each, explaining that you did this for all applications. This will prepare them for negotiations.

Or, use the Universal Application and Authorizations in the Appendix. Copy and enlarge these pages. If you wish a full size, blank copy of these forms, send a stamped, self-addressed envelope to the author. (See the order form at the back of the book.)

If you use these Universal Authorizations, you won't have to read the providers' forms — or worry that you signed away precious rights. Simply add providers names to the Universal Authorizations.

In addition:

• Some applications require notarized signatures. If you can't afford to pay for this, phone the provider. Usually they will send you a check for the cost (a tiny expense to them).

• Providers want a copy of your life insurance policy and driver's license. Send a copy of every page of the policy. If you have group insurance, send a copy of the Benefit Handbook.

• All providers ask about bankruptcy. The reason: Bankruptcy law allows creditors to go after funds received by a debtor within a specified time after the bankruptcy action. This time period varies by state, but generally is 180 days post-bankruptcy. This is important. You don't want to get a viaticum at a time when it can be claimed by creditors.

Next step:

• Notify your physicians to expect requests for the last two years' medical records. This is where the greatest delay often occurs — especially if each request arrives on a separate day. But if your doctors' staff prepares the exact number of copies all at once, it will save them time and allow for a prompt response.

> Some doctors use a copy service, which bills providers directly.This service is usually a once-weekly affair, which may delay the viatical process.
> Consider copying your own records to send to providers.

Also, alert your doctor to expect a medical questionnaire from each viatical provider. This questionnaire asks physicians for their life expectancy estimate and — more importantly — to attest to your mental competency.

• Advise your doctors to send two years' medical records,

even if providers ask for one year. According to Per Larson, the fatter the file the fatter the viatical settlement.

Now you wait. This wait may be as short as two weeks — or it may stretch out to several months.

Average time: Six weeks.

Things to Watch for:

1. Low-ball offers to snag the unwary.
2. Limited time offers.
3. Discounting or denial of tax liability.
4. Efforts to get you to sign an open-ended "hunting license" contract.
(The offer is made, signed, & <u>then</u> funding is sought. This tactic, which is common to most unlicensed firms, could keep you in limbo for 60 days or more.)
5. Problems & delays <u>after</u> signing.
(Sudden fees and other extra charges.)
6. Breeches of confidentiality.

adapted fr.<u>Viatication Guidelines</u>, Per Larson, Sept. 1994.

The Offer:

- Most offers are initiated by phone — in spite of your adding "written offers only." If the offer is by phone, insist it be put in writing. A refusal could mean they lack cash on hand to back up the offer.

- Keep in mind, this is a Seller's market. Resist the temptation to grab the first offer. Let them know you intend to compare their offer with others. This usually results in offers being raised.

- Allow for a second go-round. Providers who have

sufficient funds to raise their bid are likely to ask for written proof of the highest bid. Give it to them. If using a broker, negotiations will be handled for you.

Next step:

- You accept an offer.
- Transfer of ownership papers are zapped to you by overnight courier, along with a postage paid return envelope.
- Transfer documents usually require beneficiaries to sign a waiver of interest. This is particularly true if you have a spouse and/or children.
- Transfer documents usually require a trip to the notary.
- Return the papers using the same speedy courier.

> Licensed viatical providers must
> deposit your funds with
> an escrow company. You should
> receive written confirmation
> of this from the escrow trustee.

- Once the papers are received by the provider, you should get notice from the escrow trust that your funds are on deposit.
- Another wait — for confirmation of the recorded transfer. Usual time: 10 — 15 days. Funds should be in your bank within 48 hours of this notice.

How do funding firms decide on a purchase price?

The purchase price is determined primarily as the result of

medical and insurance *underwriting*. Underwriting is the process of putting a price tag on risk. In this case, the buyer assumes risk about your personal health and the insurer's financial health. This two-prong process is similar to underwriting for auto insurance: evaluating a person and evaluating property.

Medical evaluation is designed to answer two questions:

- What is the projected life expectancy?
- Is the person of sound mind and capable of executing this contract?

How is medical underwriting done?

It begins with your medical records and your physician. Although your personal physician is asked to estimate your life expectancy, this is not an exact science. It's not unusual for one set of medical underwriters to hold a vastly different opinion from that of your personal physician, or from medical consultants at other funding firms.

> "The medical environment changes every three months: new medical interventions, prophylactics, and so on.
> — Scott Wilbanks, broker
> (Wilbanks and Associates)

Some brokers do their own, cursory underwriting. They claim this helps them match viators with funding firm guidelines. Oh, sure. A person with no medical training makes an "educated" guess about life expectancy.

On the other hand, funding firms must be diligent — and conservative — about medical underwriting. It's their money on the line. This is why most funding firms use consultant physicians who have extensive experience treating the various diseases accepted by that provider.

ViatiCare uses outside consultants working in tandem with the viator's attending physician. At Lifetime Options, medical records are scrutinized by a staff member at Georgetown University Hospital. This doctor makes an estimate of life expectancy, suggests an offer in the range of 77-79 percent of face value, and passes the records to two other physicians, one at Walter Reed Military Medical Center, the other at the National Institutes of Health. It's the latter two who make the final offer determination.

Page & Associates uses a medical team from an utilization review company, Health Care Strategies, of Baltimore, Maryland. The Viaticum Fund uses physicians from Louisiana State University School of Medicine. These faculty members specialize in infectious disease, oncology, cardiology and neurological disorders such as ALS (Lou Gehrig's Disease).

What is legal competency?

For the viatical process, legal competency can best be described as:

> ". . . the ability to understand in a general way the nature and extent of the property to be disposed of, one's relationship to those who would naturally claim a substantial benefit from the will, and the practical effect of

> the will as executed."[2]

Although "ability to understand" is key, "practical effect" is equally important. A client who is unable to manage a large sum, or likely to fall victim to a scam, or to squander and neglect real needs, would not be considered legally competent.

If a viator isn't of sound mind, or is incapable of executing a contract, most viatical providers won't take the risk of contracting with that client. The reason: dispossessed beneficiaries may sue the provider to recover their inheritance.

But some funding firms accept alternatives:

- Power of Attorney

Some funding firms will accept an application signed by a guardian who has been appointed to have legal authority and to take charge of the client's financial affairs.

- Another expert

When a personal physician holds strong views against viatication and refuses to attest to a patient's competency, another expert may be found for substantiation. John Warburton (Life Entitlements) described one such situation:

> "We were processing an individual's policy, when we realized the doctor had signed all the forms except for the one with the question about competency. We contacted the doctor (a top AIDS doctor in New York), and asked him: 'Is your patient competent to make this decision?'
>
> "The doctor said that he did not believe it was in the best interests of a terminally ill patient to do this.
>
> "It wasn't the first time we had a doctor who had a

paternalistic attitude toward patients. I had our medical director phone the physician, hoping that one doctor speaking to another would make the difference. It turned out that the physician did not like our applicant and although the viator did not have dementia, the doctor was unwilling to affirm that he was legally competent.

"I phoned a number of psychiatrists in the area where the applicant lived, and found one who would test him for legal competency. This is a special test — a legal competency test for which the company paid. Despite this, our medical director didn't want to buy the policy. Two weeks later, the guy sold his policy to another company willing to take the risk."

What is involved in Insurance Underwriting?

An insurer's financial stability is critical. No one wants to own a policy from an Executive Life look-alike (that California life insurer that went belly-up a few years back). But financial stability can be readily determined — by checking the insurer's rating with an independent rating service such as A.M. Best, Standard & Poor's, or Moody's.

Other questions are stickier:

- Is there anything in this policy that will allow the insurer to refuse payment when the viator dies? (Example: Death occurred during the incontestability period.)

- Is there anything in this policy that will allow the insurer to reduce the death benefit? (Example: conversion caps. For details, see Chapters 1 and 7.)

- If this is a group policy, does it permit transfer of ownership and/or beneficiary?

For personally owned policies, underwriters need a copy of the latest annual statement as well as a copy of every page of the policy. For employee or association group insurance, underwriters need a copy of the Benefit Handbook. These documents help answer the above questions.

What other factors influence the offer?

Although medical and insurance underwriting are paramount, several other factors may increase or decrease settlement offers:

+ Cash values that could be used to increase the death benefit for Universal or Variable life policies

+ Guaranteed Insurability Options that may be used to increase the death benefit for cash value (whole life) policies

— Loans and loan interest (which increase cost and reduce death benefits)

+ Premium waiver on a disabled insured

— Future premiums (if there is no disability waiver of premium)

— The provider's overhead and administrative expenses

+/— Interest rates for investments bearing similar risk

+/— Availability of funds (the firm's cash flow)

Note: No charges should be made for broker commissions or referral fees. Even if your state doesn't require it, you can request disclosure of all fees.

Low-ball offers

When offers start coming in, play cool. Initial offers rarely are final offers, especially if providers know you've applied to other funding firms. Prices have increased over the years, but as recently as six months ago, a California funder made an offer of 25 percent. Since this may happen, you'd best be on your toes.

Then there are funding firms that strictly abide by regulations — compliance that extends not only to the letter but also the spirit of the law. Rather than make a low-ball offer, they'll decline to make any offer. This is why Bradley Rutter, one of the principals at Dignity Partners, views state-mandated minimums as "price restriction."

> "Mandated minimums — such as those from people with longer life expectancies — limit the ability of funding firms to buy riskier policies."
> — Bradley Rutter (Dignity Partners)

The fact that funding firms are likely to increase their offers on the second "go round" may have nothing to do with you. It may be cash flow. They may have gotten a bank credit line within days of making their initial offer; or a policy may have paid off. Now, they're able to play rough in the bidding war.

What if all offers are less than 50 percent of face value?

My guess: Your life expectancy is too long for these companies to assume the risk. Don't sell. If you're sorely in need of funds, consider alternatives (see Chapter 9).

How long until pay day?

Most firms promise payment within 48 hours of receiving notice of the transfer of ownership. But this may be two weeks or more from the day you actually signed transfer papers. During this time you're in a kind of financial limbo. You no longer own your asset, yet have nothing to show for it.

In regard to unlicensed firms, "When is Pay Day?" is one of life's big mysteries. If they're out on a hunt for funds, you might be put off for months (see Chapter 5).

What if I change my mind?

Both sides are free to change their minds anytime during the viatication process. Early on, there's no contract, no obligation whatsoever. At the other extreme, one funding firm actually canceled their offer after transfer papers were mailed to the viator. While this may be unethical, it's not illegal.

If you want to cancel after receiving the funds, you have a grace period of 15 days (in Kansas, 30 days). During that time you may change your mind without giving a reason — you won a lottery, or a dragging-its-feet viatical provider suddenly came in with a heap more money . . . any reason.

What must I do to cancel?

After receiving the funds, simply return the entire principal. Use a bank check. Send it by certified mail with a return receipt (proof it was received by the viatical provider).

But don't wait until you have the settlement to read the fine print in the contract. Several providers require reimbursement of premiums they paid to your insurer. This is fair. Another firm requires that you send them any interest earned by these funds while they were in your account. This, too, is fair — as long as they don't determine the interest rate you *should* have gotten. But not all cancellation terms are fair.

In addition to return of the viatical settlement, some funding firms charge what they call "a handling fee." How much is this handling fee? Who knows? It's not specified in the contract. Is it exorbitant? If it's steep enough to impair your right to cancel, it's illegal and therefore unenforceable.

In that case, simply send back the viaticum. If they phone to harass you, burp in their ear. Viatical law is on your side.

> **One firm charges an unspecified sum — to compensate for lost interest while the funds were in your possession.**
> **This clause might be unenforceable, if the fee impairs your right to cancel.**

It's far simpler to deal with complications like these when you apply. If you see a notice of unfair cancellation fees in the closing papers, notify the provider about your objection and cross out that paragraph. Initial the change, and ask them to initial a copy and return it to you. They may not comply, but you have served warning.

A few viatical firms permit cancellation at "no cost." Others fail to mention any cost — including reimbursement of premiums they paid on your behalf. Since funding firms pay premiums a year in advance, these firms may be short changing themselves. No doubt this failure to mention reimbursement is be an oversight — one that will be corrected as soon as someone at those firms reads this paragraph.

What are the reasons for canceling?

- Poor or no planning
- Advice from family and/or friends
- Unexpected financial assistance
- Unexpected loan
- Discovery of insurer's Accelerated Death Benefits
- Any combination of the above
- Another viatical provider finally joined the game — with a higher offer

What is meant by poor planning?

Some clients view viatical settlements as "found money" . . . as lottery winnings. And they back out when the viatical process becomes stressful.

Poor planning also means, It's the wrong time to sell. To determine if this is the wrong time for you, see the checklist at the end of Chapter 9.

Whatever you decide, don't try to go it alone. Follow Per Larson's advice. Get assistance ". . . in the form of administrative and psychological support, and technical and business skills."

* * *

END NOTES

1. A committee from the Viatical Association of America is planning a simplified, one-page application that will become standard for the industry.

2. West's Legal Thesaurus/Dictionary, William P. Statsky. West Publishing Co., St. Paul, MN, 1985.

CHAPTER 5

Licensing: Boon or Bane?

Some form of viatical regulation exists in more than a dozen states. Yet, abuses continue, bringing irretrievable harm to terminally ill people and their families. What's wrong with viatical regulation? Does it go far enough? Or does it go too far?

Tales from Cowboy Country

"Welcome to a wild west industry, that rewrites its own rules regularly."[1]

This is how Per Larson, an advocate for the terminally ill, views the viatical settlement industry. And Larson should know. He's been observing the industry since pre-regulation days, when viatical companies had names like "The Grim Reaper."

The Grim Reaper had good company: Credit Life, Corporation, which opened for business with absolutely no funds, no credit, no means whatsoever to buy policies. Nevertheless, Credit Life, with unabashed boldness, solicited viators, made purchase offers, took ownership of policies . . . and did just about everything you would expect of a funding firm. Everything, that is, except pay up.[2]

These were not isolated practices. There were funding firms and brokers that made offers, then scrambled for funds. This money hunt often took many months.

> Regarding viators who sold policies to Credit Life, John Warburton says, "Those terminally ill people lost six to nine months before they got their policies back." And Warburton knows whereof he speaks. His company, Life Entitlements, was one of the firms that purchased those policies on the second go-round.

Among the viators was a man named Adam Tillis, who had to wait five months before he saw a dime — and then it was 30 percent of face value.[3] Another man, a New Yorker with AIDS, waited an entire year for Pay Day.[4]

Not one of the early-day stories are better. There were funding firms that promised lump sum payments. But viators who suffered dementia were paid only a small portion — as if dementia would prevent these viators from knowing they had been ripped off.

And there was Tom Holtz, founder of the Dayton, Ohio-based Q-Foil Inc. Holtz saw that most viatical firms concentrated their marketing efforts on people with short life expectancies. People with longer life expectancies — as long as three and a half to five years — were ignored. Holtz targeted this group.

And was he ever on the mark! Viators accepted Q-Foil's offers: 25% of face value. According to writer Andrew Gluck, "That means that someone whose heirs could expect $100,000 when he dies, might receive $25,000 today from Holtz. And that's not an unusual discount in the viatical settlement industry."[5]

Holtz wasn't the stingiest tightwad. Other funding firms paid as little as 20 cents on the dollar.[6]

Meanwhile, investors who bought these policies were promised 20% and higher returns — promises which were kept.[7]

In those years, says John Warburton (Life Entitlements), the viatical industry was "very cowboy-like." No fences. Shoot from the hip. Anything goes. OK Corral.

Or, in Per Larson's view: "a bizarre bazaar."

> "Four years ago," writes journalist Pamela Sherrid, "someone with less than a year to live might have gotten only 40 percent of the death benefit; the going rate these days is 70 to 80 percent."

US News & World Report 8/21/95

These stories may be history . . . but they're not as ancient as the dinosaur age. Or Billy the Kid, for that matter. In fact, the viatical industry is very much a child. It's birth occurred in

1988, when a New Mexico financial planner founded Living Benefits, the first funding firm.[8] By the close of 1989, there were two more funding firms. With a grand total of three, with no regulation, with hundreds — then thousands — of young people dying of plague, it was a situation ripe for abuse.

At last the media shrugged off their uncommon lethargy. They went out to investigate. And scurried back to their dens, to pound out stories of a new industry that was both "ghoulish" and "grisly."

Despite viatical providers' fondness for describing themselves as socially conscious investors, the media were revolted. They saw a few shrewd and greedy men who gained instant wealth from the misery of terminally ill people. As for these so-called "investments" — they were nothing more than "Death Notes."

Or, "Death Futures."

> Pay Now
> (and Pay the Insured),
> or Pay Later
> (and Pay an Investor).

Pay Now or Pay Later

All this media attention opened the eyes of the insurance industry. Until now, insurers were blissfully unaware that the AIDS pandemic had wrought the creation of the viatical industry, and caused its phenomenal growth. Insurers' complacency also stemmed from a belief they had done all in their power to ease the plight of AIDS victims.

In 1984, when the AIDS crisis began, insurers committed $1.6 million dollars to AIDS related projects — to research and community-based service groups. Over the next nine years this sum grew to more than $36 million dollars.[9] Then there were AIDS-related life insurance claims, expected to top $25 billion by the mid-1990's. And another $17 billion in AIDS-related health insurance claims.[10] Despite these efforts, the viatical industry forced insurers to admit they hadn't done nearly enough.

Of the millions in death benefits insurers paid out, most went into the pockets of investors; insureds saw no more than 20 or 30 cents of each dollar. And the rightful heirs? Zilch.

It was clear: the insurance industry needed to do more for their terminally ill insureds. But what? Innovation was stymied by a labyrinth of regulations, both federal and state. Most worrisome: If pre-death benefits were paid from life insurance, would policies lose their favored tax status?[11]

This weighed heavily as the head honchos of the giant insurers gathered at the conference table, hoping for a solution. They knew the concept of paying pre-death benefits to a terminally ill insured was not entirely innovative nor radical. Endowment policies had done exactly that for years. But these were not endowment policies. Hours passed . . . and the yellow pads that lined the conference table remained unmarked.

At last a voice from the corner piped up. It was the proverbial nerd, complete with electrified hair and specs thick as cocktail table glass: "What about *the 'maturity value disability clause'*? You know: The one written with employee group term life."

Papers rustled. Head honchos pawed frantically through their manuals. One man found it, and read aloud:

"The maturity value type of disability

> clause provides for the payment of the face amount of an employee's group term life insurance in a lump sum or, more often, in monthly installments when an employee becomes totally and permanently disabled prior to age sixty."[12]

Aha! Precedent! A foundation upon which to build a rider that paid pre-death benefits!

> The ADB would pay dollar for dollar. In addition, insureds could use a percentage and leave the balance for dependents.

Thus, as the new decade began, the major insurers prepared to bring forth their own creation: Accelerated Death Benefits. It would be added by rider, or built into new contracts. It would pay death benefits to terminally ill insureds, and it would pay for long-term care. In every way Accelerated Death Benefits would be superior to viatical settlements. Insureds would not have to lose thousands to the steep discounts of viatical providers. Instead, they would get the present value of the future sum that would have been paid to heirs after death. Insurers could give a golden ring to their insureds and lose nothing by doing this: There would be minimal cost.

Minimal cost, since there was no underwriting expense; attending physicians' reports would suffice. Minimal cost, since no commissions would be paid to agents. Moreover, funds were at hand to pay this benefit. Insurers were mandated by law to maintain specified amounts in reserve, so that policy surrenders and death claims could be paid with ten days notice.

Different insurers developed different designs. Some required the rider to be added to policies before diagnosis. Others added it at any time, upon request. Some added it to newly issued policies. Others extended it to existing policies, as well. Some charged a nominal fee to add the rider; others charged a fee only if it was used. Some paid out benefits when life expectancy was six months; others at nine months, a few at twelve months, and one or two went out as far as twenty-four months. Some capped the payout at 25% of the death benefit; some allowed 50%; some went as high as 92%, or 100%. Some set dollar amounts.

> Prudential was first to offer ADB, nearly 100 percent of the death benefit.
> Connecticut Mutual followed, adding the rider to existing policies as well as new issues.

The head honchos shook hands, patted each other's backs, and returned to their traditional duties. Not one thought was given to getting the message to insureds about this new benefit. Nor did anyone wonder if insurance agents, in the absence of financial incentives, would bother to learn about this rider. Or trouble themselves to convey the news to clients.

Since no one thought to initiate a media campaign to alert the public to the new benefit, the playing field was left clear for viatical firms.[13]

And so they trooped on — with trumpets blaring, banners

waving, taking to the airwaves, chatting it up on television and talk radio, taking out full page color ads in gay publications — at $4,000 a pop. One viatical funding firm, Accelerated Benefits of Washington, spent $40,000 on advertising in its first year.

When NAIC speaks

By the close of 1993, IRS had new regulations for insurers that offered Accelerated Death Benefits.[14] By contrast, the viatical industry was completely unregulated, a bizarre bazaar. Except that now there were forty viatical firms, and as many horror stories. It was at this point that the insurance industry's watchdog, the National Association of Insurance Commissioners, flexed its muscles.

NAIC drafted model regulations for states to use when designing their own viatical laws.[15] California, the renown innovator, was first to implement regulation. Viatical contracts were placed under the supervision of the Department of Insurance; licensees were required to comply with a number of consumer safeguards. Chief among the safeguards: medical confidentialty. This provision continues to be of particular importance: at least one unlicensed provider routinely violates medical confidentially.[16] (For details, see Chapter 6).

Additional requirements include:

- Disclosure to viators of possible alternatives to viatical settlements contracts including, but not limited to, accelerated benefits options that may be offered by the life insurer
- Disclosure of tax consequences
- Disclosure of the consequences for interruption of public assistance

• Disclosure to viators of their absolute right to rescind (cancel) the contract within 15 days of execution. "Any waiver or contract language contrary to this subdivision shall be void."[17]

• Viatical providers must offer proof of financial stability. To meet this requirement, licensees must submit a number of items to the Insurance Department, including:

• Details of the viatical firm's financial resources with CPA audited financial statements

• Detailed descriptions listing life expectancies in 6 month intervals showing:

— criteria used to determine the discount rate paid for policies

— other factors that effect this payment

— a Discount Rate Table up to and including a 24 month life expectancy

• Description of how payment is made to viators:

— lump sum

— installments

— timing of payments

— how and why payment is held back or put aside for later payment

• Details of the escrow/trust account procedures used to:

— ensure that the entire viaticum will be immediately paid to the viator

— prevent mismanagement of Applicant's funds

— ensure that there are sufficient monies to back the offer

Providers must establish an escrow account at a "qualified,

licensed financial institution," and provide the DOI with the names of these financial institutions.

There's more, but these are the essential features. Sounds good, doesn't it? Now for the $64,000 dollar question: Do these regulations work?

Pros and Cons

Alan Perper, one of the founders of *Dignity Partners* and a staunch supporter of viatical regulation, vigorously denounces one aspect of regulation:

"Price restrictions. They are overbearing, especially for people with longer life expectancies. If I have to pay a certain amount and it's more than I think it's worth, I won't buy, and people lose out."

Other than price restriction, Perper finds little fault with California's laws. New York is another story:

> "New York makes life difficult. The paperwork is overwhelming — different from regulations in other states. And it's costly to comply. They're constantly sending out memos that change the rules. First they had a requirement that we tell viators their life expectancy. New York's attitude is paternalistic — too much so. Some viators don't want to know their life expectancy. Then New York revised the life expectancy disclosure. With another memo: Tell only if requested by viators."

Some providers are vehement about one aspect of California's regulations: the apparent fixation with dual licensing. The most extreme example is the story behind the licensing efforts of Nancy Cane, the broker who founded *Benefit Advocates*.

Cane's brokerage got stuck in pending status for well over two years — while she feuded with the DOI. Cane, who was an insurance agent before switching to the viatical industry, didn't want to surrender her insurance license. Although she had no intention of selling insurance, surrender of the insurance license meant the loss of renewal and service fees earned through the years. The issue was finally resolved in late 1995: Cane kept her insurance license but was listed as "inactive," and her brokerage was granted its viatical license.

Don't expect any changes in this regard: Cane's problem is not common. There are few principals in the viatical industry who have insurance backgrounds. Instead, most start out in total ignorance, and get training in insurance contracts and insurance law while "on the job." Several of these once-ignorant viatical providers view this as daunting — as evidenced by the provider who advised me not to attempt a book on viatical settlements. "It's much too complicated," I was told. "You'll never understand. And everything changes quickly."

> Cane's problem reveals two flaws in the California regulation:
> (1) No requirement that licensees have insurance knowledge, and
> (2) A disincentive for those who are knowledgeable to enter the viatical industry.

California's view of insurance agents as dangerous to viators contrasts markedly with the approach taken by Washington state. In Washington applicants for viatical licenses must pass the state insurance exam. They aren't issued insurance licenses. Instead, the exam is used to demonstrate that licensees have a basic knowledge of insurance contracts and insurance law.

California's predilection for ignorance is at the bottom of the list of problems at the DOI. The agency might have stacks of evidence against a violator, but the worst offense is nothing more serious than a misdemeanor — like trespassing. The steepest penalty — fines up to ten thousand dollars — is but a drop in the ole bucket, compared to the profit potential from a single life insurance policy.

Fly-by-night companies have it easy: no fees to pay; no reports to file; no authorities poking around, controlling their advertising.[18] The most serious penalty — suspension or revocation of a viatical license — doesn't make them flinch: they have no license to lose. Thus, a thriving underground of illegal companies operates right under the nose of the DOI.

More than a year ago the DOI received evidence of a front organization for Brian Pardo's Life Partners (see Chapter 6). At this writing, the front organization continues to be on the DOI's license-pending list, and operates in California. When asked about this, the DOI claimed, "The matter is under investigation."

At this writing at least four other illegal companies are buzzing around California, soliciting viatical contracts or lining up investors. When a client told me she had applied to sell her policy to a viatical firm that I knew was not on the DOI list, I reported them to the DOI. I was told that Medical Escrow Society had applied for a license and been refused, and agreed not to do business in California. The story ends here. The viator withdrew her application but didn't file a complaint, and the

DOI had no cause to investigate.

Another illegal company actively solicites California investors to buy the life insurance policies of terminally ill people — and promises a return of "at least 42 percent."[19]

And another: Washington Viatical Network, Inc., a broker based in Olney, Maryland, uses the U.S. Postal Service to lure viators. Then there's Lancaster Annuity Services Company (Naperville, Illinois), also using the USPS, this time to solicit insurance agents to line up investors. Agents are tempted with promises of 6 percent commissions. Lancaster Annuity's promotional materials specifically state that securities and insurance licenses are "NOT required." Which is particularly peculiar, since Lancaster Annuity advertises itself as offering securities through Long Grove Trading Company, a member of the National Association of Securities Dealers (NASD).

Then there's Accelerated Benefits Corp. of Winter Park, Florida (not to be confused with Accelerated Benefits Capital of Michigan, which legally operates in the states of Washington, California, and Texas). The illegal "ABC" solicits both ends of the viatical industry: insurance agents to sell policies as investments, and viators with life insurance policies. The illegal "ABC" is aligned with Universal Concepts Marketing Enterprise and National Exchange, Inc., both of which work out of the very same office at Royal Palm Beach, Florida. This conglomerate also conducts seminars; their seminar schedule includes visits to sites in North Carolina and to Newport Beach, Virginia.

That "illegals" proliferate in states like California is due not only to weak enforcement by the DOI, but also to viators who sell policies to them. Aren't viators aware of the risks?

No, they're not. I have yet to speak with a viator who ever heard of such an animal as viatical regulation — never mind licensing laws. Viators don't know their rights. They don't know if they are being cheated or treated abusively. And if they smell something fishy, for obvious reasons people who are terminally ill are highly likely to register formal complaints.

Nor is their problem relieved by turning to professional advisors. Few attorneys, tax professionals, or social workers have more knowledge than their terminally ill clients.

The situation is bad — and could get worse. Couple lack of enforcement with the expense (and hassle) of applying for a license, and one has to wonder why any viatical firm submits to regulation.

Or do they?

> "California can't enforce regulations because the DOI hasn't the funds to do this."
> — Robert Shear
> (Accelerated Benefits Capital)

A few viatical firms send in the required paperwork, pay the fee (nearly 3 thousand dollars), then ignore viatical regulations. They know the DOI won't yank licenses unless they have a tower of evidence — evidence they can't get without an investigation. An investigation they can't do without funds.

Insufficient funding is the root of just about every problem at the DOI. Yet, on occasion the DOI has acted effectively: Three companies that applied for licenses were banned from operating within the state. According to a DOI spokesperson:

> "These companies misled clients, and in more than one case were slow to pay. The latter is of particular concern, given that viaticals deal with patients who generally have less than two years to live."

More recently (the summer of 1995), the California DOI clamped down on *Viaticus*, the heavy-weight funding firm owned by giant insurer CNA. The reason: Viaticus's newly-launched marketing campaign to secure referrals from people they termed "*intermediaries*." These intermediaries included:

- Clergy & Social Workers connected with church groups
- Visiting Nurse Associations (AIDS and oncology nurses)
- Hospitals (nurses, discharge planners, case managers)
- Home Infusion and Respiratory Therapy Professionals
- Hospice and Nursing Home Administrators
- Local community groups that serve patients with cancer, heart, and other life threatening illnesses.[20]

Viaticus hungered for referrals from all "centers of influence," but was ravenous for the clients of insurance agents. To lure agents to direct terminally ill clients to Viaticus — rather than inform them about insurers' ADB — referral fees were offered. And not only to sales agents, but to General Agents who administrate insurance offices — to encourage the staff to make these referrals.

When the DOI pulled their license, Viaticus, eager to regain it, agreed to halt their California campaign. They also promised never to do such a dastardly deed again. Leastwise, not in the Golden State.

Despite these instances, DOI efforts to protect viators don't begin to compare with the efforts of fire fighters to save residents of a burning building. But if you think California's general economic turmoil makes this state unique, think again. According to Jane Bryant Quinn, financial journalist for Newsweek and The Washington Post, this is a malady common to most states.

> "The public record probably won't include pending actions or customer complaints. Those are usually kept on a separate list, for only the regulators to see. Your agent could come up clean on paper, yet be a weasel underneath."[21]

Quinn was referring to insurance departments in general, but her words apply equally to oversight of viatical contracts.

Two other issues: In January 1996 I phoned the DOI's consumer hotline to request the latest list of viatical licensees. I was sent a list dated August 1995 — five months old. I'm told that the list is updated daily. Later, when I advised a viator to phone for the list, she was sent one that was three months old . . .. Progress?

Another viator phoned the hotline to ask if his insurer was adding the ADB rider to existing policies. He spoke to a DOI staffer who hadn't the foggiest notion what Bill was talking about. After a few grunts, the staffer asked if the viator was calling to register a complaint, and sent him complaint forms — but no information about the insurer's ADB. Nor did he send the DOI's two-page memo on viatical contracts. More's the pity, since the memo — which advises viators to seek at least three bids — is one thing that the state does well. It's free for the asking — but you won't get it unless you ask. Phone 1-800-927-

HELP if you live within the state; outside California, phone 1-213-897-8921.

* * *

END NOTES

1. "Living Benefits from Life Insurance," Per Larson. Victory, January/February 1995.

2. Legal action by Florida's attorney general eventually reversed these policies back to their original owners.

3. Tillis is co-founder of ViatiCare.

4. "AIDS Spawns Viatical Settlement Industry," Amy Keller. Washington Business Journal, Sept. 23-29, 1994.

5. "The Trouble with Pennies from Heaven," Andrew Gluck. Worth, July/Aug. 1993.

6. "Merchants of Death Benefits Get New Rules," Susan Harrigan. New York Newsday, Aug. 4, 1994.

7. "New Industry Earning 20% on Terminally Ill," Carey Gillam. Kansas Business Journal, May 28-June 3, 1993.

8. Living Benefits now is owned by National Capital Benefits, the first publicly-traded funding firm. National Capital also owns and funds American Life Resources.

9. II*Can, the Insurance Industry's Citizen Action Network publication, Summer 1995.

10. "The Impact of AIDS on the Insurance Industry," Getz, Kenneth A, and Bentkover, Judith D. Journal of the American Society of CLU and ChFC, March 1992.

11. Life insurance death benefits are tax free to beneficiaries, and the inside build-up of cash values is tax free.

12. "Group Insurance I," Noble Continuing Education. Noble Financial Group, Inc., Houston, TX, 1995.

13. Lincoln National Life includes on every annual statement for Universal Life the following paragraph:

"Lincoln National's Accelerated Benefit Election Rider allows you the option of electing a Death Benefit advance in the event the insured person is diagnosed as having a terminal illness. **This rider can be added to your policy with no increase in cost of insurance.** Please ask your agent or service representative for more information." (sic)

14. "The Taxation of Accelerated Benefits Under a Life Insurance Contract," Griffin, Mark E. Journal of the American Society of CLU and ChFC, July 1993.

15. The Wall Street Journal, Dec. 7, 1993.

16. Article 6. § 791 et seq. of Chapter 1 of Part 2 of Division 1.

17. California Insurance Code § 10113.1 et seq., and California licensing application for viatical contracts.

18. Life Insurance, eleventh edition, Black, Jr., Kenneth and Skipper, Jr., Harold. Prentice-Hall, 1987.

19. Reported to the author by several sources. This company is not named, since I have no direct evidence to support this allegation. Illegal companies are named only when there is evidence to support the charge.

20. The source of this information is marketing materials sent to insurance brokers by Viaticus.

21. "Where Are They Now?" Quinn, Jane Bryant. Newsweek, August 21, 1995.

CHAPTER 6

Grateful for AIDS:

The Brian Pardo Story

He's the president of Life Partners Inc., and a major player in the new viatical industry. But he's considered "one of its blackest sheep," "a rogue," "an outlaw," and "a merchant of death." Apparently nothing will stop Brian Pardo. Nothing but a cure for AIDS.

Victor L. was one of many AIDS patients who sold his life insurance to Life Partners Inc. of Waco, Texas. Victor didn't know Life Partners's history: that it had been accused of conducting a scam, that Life Partners's in-house physician determined life expectancy, that this physician had absolutely no experience in the treatment of AIDS. He didn't know that Dr.

John Kelly's sole qualification for this important decision was ownership of 5,000 shares of Life Partners' stock.[1]

Dr. Kelly predicted Victor's life expectancy as 24 to 36 months. Eight months later, Victor died — unaware that he had been cheated out of thousands of dollars. Nor did he know his life insurance had been resold by Life Partners — to twelve individuals scattered cross the face of the nation.

When the dozen owners learned that Victor's policy had "matured," they were ecstatic: The return on their investment was an astronomical 66.67 percent! Typical returns for investors of these policies were in the range of 15 to 20 percent, but LPI investors hoped for more. After all, no less a personage than LPI's president, Brian Pardo, had said "the policies can sometimes result in more spectacular payoffs of as much as 80 percent."[2]

And then some. After Life Partners (LPI) resold 100 policies worth almost $2 million to The Lanrick Group, one of those investors had an 86% return. The reason: "A patient lived nine rather than the 36 months."[3]

> "We don't buy a policy until they have a diagnosis of full-blown AIDS," says Pardo. "We know then that they have at the most twenty-four months to live — it is a death certificate."

"Grim Reaping," Helen Thompson, Texas Monthly. Nov. 1992

Nor are these isolated cases. Among LPI's marketing materials is a chart comparing life expectancy estimates with actual time to date of death. Of 80 viators listed, not one policy yielded a return below 11 percent; 27 were in excess of 20 percent; three had yields over 65 percent.

These huge profits suggest that "in-house physician" Dr. Kelly fabricates unrealistically long life expectancies, in order to ensure good returns to investors. But the opposite is equally true. Occasionally, AIDS patients get higher offers from LPI than from industry standard-bearers like Dignity Partners, Accelerated Benefits Capital (Michigan), American Life Resources, or Legacy Benefits.

These heavily-financed funding firms periodically lose sales to Pardo. It may be that Dignity Partners offers 80 percent, but Life Partners will offer 83 percent. For a policy with a face value of $100,000, this is a difference of $3,000. And viators don't know the first thing about LPI. The extra thousands scream in their ears. No one tells them what will happen to their medical records.

In Robert Shear's view (Accelerated Benefits Capital), LPI intentionally overpays viators — in order to corner the viatical market.

> "Something's wrong when independent medical advisors for three funding firms judge life expectancy as between 12 and 18 months, and Pardo comes in with an estimate of 9 months. Something's wrong, but Pardo *isn't concerned about* overpaying. This is investor money — not his own. He doesn't care if investors overpay. He gets his spread up front. When viators don't die on time and investors get upset, Pardo talks it away by telling them about viators who died in half the time."

Shear and others claim that Pardo's unrealistic high bids are harming the viatical industry. First, these bids artificially raise prices. Secondly, licensed firms can't compete with unlicensed ones, since it's more costly to comply with regulation and since their practices are closely watched. This, in turn, could drive legitimate providers out of business. More important, when Pardo over-pays, he manipulates investors. Eventually, these disgruntled investors may raise such a ruckus that they'll cause the money supply to dry up.

Similar complaints were voiced by other funding firms. But they don't know — and viators don't learn until too late — that LPI's offers only *appear* to be generous. In truth, most of LPI's offers are Gross figures. Net is something else.

Net means "after expenses." Viatical regulation mandates settlement offers that are net of all expenses: What you see is what you get. But Pardo's viators rarely get every dollar of the offer. After they dismiss other buyers and sign LPI's contract, they are hit with a witch's brew of expenses.

When buyers (investors) pay
80 to 85 percent
of the death benefit,
sellers (who pay various fees) end
up with 65-70%.

Brian Pardo explains it this way: "Buyers pay 80 to 85 percent of face value in exchange for being named the policy owner." How much of this goes to sellers? In Pardo-land, "The seller is responsible for legal fees and closing costs, so the seller ends up with 65 to 70 percent of the policy's coverage value."[4]

What does this mean in real dollars? If a policy has a face value of $100,000, buyers pay 85 percent ($85,000). Sellers get 70 percent ($70,000). What happened to 15 thousand dollars?

Of course: Life Partners takes its cut. LPI admit to a fee of 5 percent ($5,000). Perhaps it's actually ten thousand, since LPI deals with numerous middle-line people. This is what Pardo terms a "win-win" situation. Buyers own a $100,000 policy for only $85,000; Life Partners collects a fee of $10,000; and viators collect only $65,000 or $70,000.

But there are occasions when viators get far less. Pardo explained:

> "In general, a $100,000 face-value holder receives $60,000, if it is estimated the person has between one and three years to live. If life expectancy is shorter, payment would probably be 61 to 63 percent, and 59 percent if the life expectancy is longer."[5]

Are Pardo's viators being cheated? Not possible. Not when one terminally ill viator has ever filed a complaint against Life Partners.

The power behind LPI

He may be a "combative, voluble businessman," but Brian Pardo looks like an average Joe in his mid-fifties: square of jaw, balding, and bespectled. Yet some see him as dapper, charismatic, and, yes, charming.

Apparently this charm is reserved for select segments of the media. Why else would so many members of The Third Estate accept without question — and without proof — Pardo's favorite song and dance routine:

- That "Life Partners Inc. is the largest viatical settlement company in the nation."[6]

The media repeats this claim like a mantra. Or perhaps journalists are simply copying one another, too lazy to do their homework. If so, it's a laziness that served Pardo well — bestowing upon him an aura of unearned respectability.

Here's another oft-repeated Pardo tune:

- That he's a broker, since Life Partners arranges transactions between sellers and buyers.

A broker unlike other brokers, LPI claims to represent the buyers — not the sellers. Unlike other brokers, LPI buys policies directly from AIDS patients, and buys directly from other brokers, or on resale, from funding firms.

Confusing, isn't it? Could it be that Pardo is a switch-hitter? Possibly. On occasion, Pardo has described Life Partners as a funding firm. He does this flip-flop with the greatest ease, totally uninhibited by viatical regulation.

But if LPI is a funding firm, it's unlike any other. Instead of holding policies, LPI bundles them for resale to investors. Which brings us to another of Pardo's theme songs:

- That he has a buyer list of 3,000 wealthy investors.

Alternately, Pardo brags that he "brought viatical transactions to the masses."[7] These "masses" connect with LPI through a radio or print ad that offers safe, high yield, humanitarian investments. Which brings us to another twist:

- Since these "masses" are not wealthy, Pardo allows them to become investors for minimal outlays of $5,000 ($2,000 for an IRA). Mind you, $5,000 doesn't buy an entire policy. It buys a piece. A "fractionalized" piece, in Pardo's words.

"Fractionalized piece"?

One insurance policy might be "fractionalized" for as many as twenty owners.

Does that smell like mutual funds?

Does a rose by any other name smell as sweet?

The Power behind the NVA

In 1994, when the viatical industry's first trade association was formed, Brian Pardo became its first president. Almost immediately, the National Viatical Association (NVA) became his mirror-image.[8] Almost immediately, Pardo set about converting the NVA into The Voice of Anti-regulation.

Pardo said, "People should have the same right to sell their insurance as they do other personally-owned property like a car or a house."[9]

> ". . . it strikes at the heart of a free market, the right of individuals to buy or sell their personal property and other constitutional rights enjoyed by all Americans."
> — Brian Pardo

And his faithful NVA chorus repeated the refrain: "We are strictly against government intervention. A life insurance policy is personal property of the owner, and buyers and sellers should be allowed to do as they please with their property . . . without

Uncle Sam's help."[10]

Pardo and his followers are using a tactic common to extremist groups (although some politicians are not above using it — to deflect public attention from real issues). This tactic demands a morsel of truth, for it's that morsel that gets listeners to swallow the whole — hook, line and sinker.

But the facts are these: Wherever viatical regulation exists, not one word is directed to regulation of viators. Rather, these laws are designed with a singular purpose — to protect the public. Particularly the most vulnerable segment of the public — people made destitute by terminal illness.

Then Pardo tried another tack:

> "Government regulation will result in increased administrative costs for viatical settlement companies. In turn, this may discourage viatical companies from buying policies in states where they are regulated. This would seriously impede the ability of any terminally ill person to sell their policy."[11]

Once again, a tidbit of truth blended with a ton of mischief. In reality, viatical providers are beating down doors to get licensed in California and New York — as well as small states like Vermont (which limits broker fees to 2 percent). By the end of January, 1996, 24 viatical firms were licensed in California (including 3 brokers), and another 11 licenses (including 2 brokers) were pending.

More and more states enacted viatical regulation, but Brian Pardo ignored them all. In defiance of law, he marched into New York and bought and sold policies. In defiance of law, he marched into California, and bought and sold policies. And he frankly admitted to a reporter that he was operating in both these states without a license.[12]

In the summer of 1995, Nancy Ayoob, a staff attorney with the California Department of Insurance, told journalist Sherrid that she suspected Pardo was buying policies in California. Ms. Ayoob added that she would move against Life Partners once she had evidence.

Getting evidence was the problem: Brian Pardo and LPI don't operate openly. They hide behind thin facades: a front organization with another name, or licensed insurance agents who, by California law, are prohibited from peddling life insurance with one hand and viatical contracts with the other.

Despite a history of abuses within the viatical industry, Pardo continued to insist, "The industry does not need outside regulators, since it can police itself."[13]

How so?

"The NVA has developed its own codes of conduct."

And just how effective are these codes?

Silence.

There are viatical providers who lock viators into taking installment payments over a set period of time. Some of these providers have "run out of money to pay for their promise, during the wait. Those are the companies that the NVA *won't talk about*."[14] (Italics added.)

Installment payments may short-change viators, but even if done honestly, this setup is illegal. It's illegal because installment payments over a set period of time are known as annuities. And viatical firms are prohibited from selling annuities. In fact, annuities are the sole provence of the highly regulated insurance industry — with good reason. Insurers are highly regulated, so much so that during the Great Depression many old line insurers like Lincoln National had the reserves to make payments on annuities contracts without a hitch.

Despite this, Pardo continues to lambaste the insurance industry. Heed his words, but don't ask the real reason behind his anger.

> "Mr. Pardo says that regulation is supported by insurance companies who want to limit viatical settlements, in hopes that more terminally ill people would run out of money and let their life insurance policies lapse before they die."[15]

This is an easy call for Pardo, since many people dislike insurers. An easy call, except that his argument doesn't hold water. For one thing, among many federal and state laws that regulate the insurance industry there is one provision that obligates insurers to provide alternatives to lapsed life insurance policies. These alternatives are described in Chapter 7.

> "[Insurers] reap millions each year when terminally ill policyholders are unable to make the premium payments to keep their policies in force."
> — Brian Pardo

Pardo's theme song also ignores the impracticality — the poor economics — of encouraging policies to lapse. It ignores the fact that insurers attempt to keep policies from lapsing by paying service fees to agents and brokers to encourage them to keep old policies on the books. Perhaps Pardo doesn't know that when a policy enters the grace period but before it lapses, insurers send an urgent request to agents to "conserve" that policy.

But Pardo had a bone between his teeth and wouldn't let go. His attacks against the insurance industry continued:

> "Although they probably won't admit it, the life insurance industry hates the viatical industry. Why? Think about it for a moment. Insurance companies in the U.S. pocketed a tidy $3 billion from policy holders who lapsed their policies during 1994 alone."[16]

Such denunciations ignored the reality that many established, licensed viatical firms have earned name recognition with insurance "giants." Thus, when these viatical firms phone insurers on behalf of a viator, insurers agree to waive incontestability clauses. Or they reinstate lapsed policies. Insurers are well aware that this leniency on their part will allow their terminally ill insureds to sell their policies.[17]

Pardo's moaning and groaning is nothing more than the old smoke-and-mirrors trick. The purpose: to hide the true identities of Pardo's enemies and strongest critics: his peers. Ethical providers don't accept his claim as the leader of the industry.

"I was a member of the NVA for one and a half hours," said Kenneth Klein, who heads two leading viatical funding firms, American Life Resources and Living Benefits. "Just long enough to go to one meeting and understand the nature of the NVA and Brian Pardo's influence and philosophy."

In January 1995, the majority of viatical providers mutinied from the NVA, leaving a scarce handful to follow Pardo. This mutiny came in the wake of a lawsuit filed against Pardo and Life Partners by the Securities Exchange Commission (SEC).

With allegations of fraud, misrepresentation, and securities violations shrouding Pardo, members of the NVA asked him to step down. Pardo refused.

> What Pardo doesn't realize — or doesn't want to admit — is that his real enemies are the ethical viatical providers.

"I realized that if the industry was to grow," said Klein, "it would have to be without Brian Pardo."

"He's a dictator," said Alan Perper of Dignity Partners. "This became obvious at meetings, the way his allies on the Board voted with him every time, the way they overturned nearly every ruling the membership had initially passed."

The defectors immediately laid plans for a second trade group, the Viatical Association of America. The VAA pledged to abide by NAIC guidelines and to support regulation. At this writing, the VAA has twenty-four members, and charges an annual membership fee of $5,000 — two hundred more than when they belonged to Pardo's NVA.

Pardo's war games

Pardo ordered his attorneys to file for an injunction to stop the proposed VAA from holding an organizational meeting without him.[18] When he lost, he instituted individual lawsuits against Alan Perper and Bradley Rutter of Dignity Partners and Meir Eliav of Legacy Benefits — industry leaders whom he considered the ringleaders of the mutiny.

Once again Pardo lost. But failure didn't dull his enthusiasm for wielding the legal system as a club in his private battles. His worthy opponents include:

- Glenn Pomeroy, North Dakota's securities commissioner
- The North American Securities Administrators Association
- M. Thomas Day II of Utah, who headed up a viatical firm
- Two reporters and their newspapers
- Metropolitan Life Insurance
- The California Department of Insurance
- California's DOI staff attorney, Nancy Ayoob

Pardo as plaintiff

In 1992, the North American Securities Administrators Association (NASA), a group of state securities regulators, issued a public warning that Life Partners was running a scam operation related to viatical settlements.[19] NASA also charged LPI with failure to properly register for the marketing of securities. And North Dakota's Securities Commissioner, Glenn Pomeroy, issued a cease and desist order to prevent Pardo from conducting viatical sales in his state.

> The scam was described by N.A.S.A. as "promising big returns to investors who bought life insurance from AIDS patients who rarely existed."

Pardo countersued Commissioner Pomeroy and NASA — charging them with slander and libel. When his lawsuit was tossed out of court, Pardo, undaunted, began his war with the National Association of Insurance Commissioners (NAIC).

NAIC hadn't done anything about Pardo — yet. But it was about to meet for the express purpose of drafting model viatical regulation. Pardo's first volley was an accusation that NAIC was "heavily influenced by the insurance industry." Such statements might be viewed as ludicrous, considering that insurers are anything but fond of NAIC. The reason: NAIC not only are state regulators in name, but police the insurance industry with tenacity.

Pardo temporarily tabled the war with NAIC, in order to direct his energies against Tom Day, a Utah-based insurance salesman.

Day had worked with Brian Pardo and LPI until the SEC filed its charges. During this time, whenever Day questioned Pardo's ethics or the legality of certain activities, Pardo put each concern to rest. But with the filing of the SEC lawsuit, Day severed his relationship with Life Partners, and set up his own viatical company — a funding firm. Although he had signed a "noncompete" agreement with Pardo, Day assumed that a funding firm would not be competition for a broker. Was he ever wrong.

Pardo sued Tom Day. Unable to finance a protracted legal battle, Day agreed to an out of court settlement: He shut down his business, and paid Pardo ten grand.[20]

Suddenly Pardo's busy year got much busier. He was called before the Federal court in Washington, D.C., to answer charges brought by the Securities Exchange Commission. While juggling Federal court with one hand, Pardo's other hand was busy threatening lawsuits against two journalists and the newspapers in which they were published.

Bob Roehr, a Washington-based journalist, had written an

account of Pardo's August 1995 Federal court hearing. The account was brief and factual, and was published in a Texas bimonthly, The Texas Triangle.[21] In addition to straight facts, Roehr described Pardo as "a rogue who refused to register with insurance commissioners in California and New York, as state law requires."

A Pardo associate dashed off a letter, demanding The Texas Triangle "retract and/or correct this blatant misstatement of fact." And there was a second demand. The editor was to provide assurance that Pardo would not be subjected to "similar treatment in the future." The letter hinted broadly at a possible suit for libel.

Such fuss and bother. It didn't reach a large audience, and it wasn't reprinted anywhere. So why the fuss and bother?

The reason: this was a Texas newspaper and "the gentleman cowboy" from Waco, Texas, was about to spring his campaign for a seat in the United States Senate. This Texas newspaper also was a gay publication, and Pardo wanted the votes of the gay community. So badly did he lust for these votes that he maneuvered to get Parker Willson, president of Waco-based Gay and Lesbian Alliance of Central Texas, to draft a letter of support — an outright endorsement. This letter became part of LPI's promotional materials, and Willson became part of Pardo's organization — executive director of Pardo's mirror-image trade group, the National Viatical Association.[22] Then, suddenly, in January, 1995, Willson was gone from the NVA: "the mysterious August resignation of its executive director, Parker Wilson."[23] Without commenting on this, Pardo took another turn on his warpath. This time it was a newspaper with a far larger readership: The Washington Blade.

In the August 4 issue, beneath the banner, "Let the Seller Beware," journalist Jose Zuniga described the viatical settlement industry and the efforts of Dennis Palmer, an AIDS patient, to sell his $60,000 life insurance policy.

Zuniga told how Palmer phoned five viatical companies, all chosen from ads in gay publications; how he succumbed to pressure and "out-and-out lying;" how he finally settled for $32,000. Then Palmer grew impatient with "'the check's in the mail' line." He phoned his insurer, only to learn the transfer of ownership papers had never been sent to them.

Palmer eventually sold his policy to another viatical provider — for $42,000, but wanted "to warn other people with AIDS of the dangers they might face in selling their life insurance."

> Palmer said, "I'm not the only one who's been burned."

Palmer's story was the lead-in to Brian Pardo and Life Partners: "Shady business dealings have landed one major national viatical settlement company in court."

The SEC investigation revealed a number of alarming facts. But journalist Zuniga also conducted a personal investigation, and quoted nearly every party, including those whose involvement was tangential (e.g., an examiner with the New York State Insurance Department). All in all, Zuniga's story was more detailed and thorough than similar accounts by the New York Times and the Wall Street Journal.

There was an immediate outcry from John McLemore, Life Partners' Director of Corporate Communications. McLemore's letter labelled the story "malicious in content," accused the Blade of "reckless disregard for the truth," and denounced the entire article as "libelous of a perfectly legal and legitimate business."

Despite the fist-pounding, McLemore blew his credibility — with a story intended to prove the "legitimacy" of Life Partners:

> "The Blade deliberately omitted the fact that the company that finally helped Dennis Palmer was Life Partners. Mr. Palmer contracted to sell his policy directly to Life Partners for the higher, market-value price."

Directly to Life Partners? Uh uh. Not exactly. In fact, Dennis Palmer "sold his policy to Page & Associates, not directly to Life Partners, Inc."

> The Blade's editor added: "Page & Associates did, subsequent to the publication of our article, acknowledge that it sold Palmer's policy to Life Partners."

In an Editor's note The Blade declared it would stand by the entire story, adding that Brian Pardo didn't return calls placed by The Blade's reporter prior to publication.

Pardo's next move came on October 10, 1995: He filed suit in federal court against Metropolitan Life, California's DOI, and DOI staff attorney, Nancy Ayoob — suing Ms. Ayoob as an individual. Pardo's suit accused MetLife, the DOI and attorney Ayoob with conspiring together to unlawfully harm Life Partners with tortious interference with the conduct of his business, and slander. Specifically, Pardo alleges that Life Partners was prevented from buying the policy of an AIDS patient insured with Metropolitan Life. This occurred, Pardo claims, as the result of Ms. Ayoob informing MetLife that LPI was not licensed to do business in California. Thus, MetLife refused to honor the transfer of ownership to LPI.[24]

The fact that Pardo is not licensed to do business in California matters not a whit; the case is pending.

> "Pardo's activities make his disdain for regulation clear. He says matter-of-factly that he does business in states like California and New York without the required licenses. When the New York Insurance Department asked Life Partners to put the disclaimer 'not available in New York' in national magazine ads, Pardo said, 'I told them to fly a kite.'"
> — Pamela Sherrid, "Enriching the Final Days"

U.S. News & World Report, August 21, 1995

Pardo on the hot seat

Pardo's war with government regulators didn't begin with his activities in the viatical industry. His resume includes:

- Conflicts with the Resolution Trust Corporation due to an unpaid loan from a failed savings and loan association.[25]

- Charges of financial fraud brought by the SEC in 1989. At that time Pardo was chief executive of a Texas-based solar utility company. He was charged with overstating the financial results of his company, which eventually went bankrupt.

The case settled out of court, with Pardo promising he would never again violate securities laws. Yet, within the blink of an eye, he was doing it again — this time as entrepreneur in the fledgling, booming viatical industry. This time Pardo was determined not to end up bankrupt. This time he would become a millionaire.

LPI opened for business in 1991. In 1992, NASA charged Pardo (and LPI) with conducting a scam related to viatical settlements, and ordered them to stop doing business.[26]

But this was the "go-fly-a-kite," business-as-usual Brian Pardo. Turning a deaf ear toward NASA, he ascended the podium of NVA, then lived through a mutiny, then waged war in the courts, and finally fielded a frontal assault from the Securities and Exchange Commission.

In 1994 the SEC charged Brian Pardo (and LPI) with securities violations, fraud and misrepresentation — all in connection with the viatical business.[27] When the results of the SEC investigation were revealed in open court, they exposed the tangled web of Life Partners, and threw into question the honesty and integrity of LPI's president, Brian D. Pardo.

The SEC v. Pardo and LPI

There were numerous securities violations that effect investors, but the bulk of misrepresentations, materially false statements, and omissions hit hardest on terminally ill viators. Among them:

- Violations of viators' confidential, private information. Copies of medical history were distributed as marketing materials for investors throughout the nation.[28]

• Medical evaluations that Life Partners claimed were done by an "independent reviewing physician." The SEC revealed that this physician was a Life Partners director and shareholder, with no particular experience in diagnosing or treating AIDS.[29] Equally important, Dr. John Kelly "also happens to own 5,000 shares in the company's stock — which might call into question his objectivity."[30]

Bobby G. Moore, insured for
$52,000 with Cigna Life Insurance,
Policy #VTL 004420000
Certificate No. 238-04-5881.
Edward C. Starkeson, insured for
$135,000 with BCS Life Insurance,
Policy #L-AD-22000
Certificate No. 328-44-3625.
John D. Bray, insured for $188,000
with MetLife,
Policy # 28822

Source: investor letters signed by B. Pardo in 1995

• The selection of Sterling Trust for the escrow account. Although escrow accounts are intended to safeguard viators' funds, Sterling Trust was not a recognized financial institution, and the trust administrator was "the son of a Life Partners' director and shareholder." The SEC revealed that neither "Junior" nor his law firm were experienced in dealing with viatical settlements.[31]

• The mystery behind Life Partners.

Pardo refused to identify the owners, except to say that 90 percent were offshore corporations.[32]

At the first hearing, the Court issued a preliminary

injunction. Brian Pardo and LPI were barred from continuing their business and were ordered to bring their operations into compliance with securities laws "forthwith."

Addressing the SEC's concern with unidentified offshore owners, the Court ordered all life insurance policies in LPI's possession turned over to a neutral third party and held "for the benefit of those investors who have purchased interests in them."[33]

The following month the Court ordered Pardo and LPI to file a statement and sworn affidavit detailing the steps taken, or which they planned to take, to comply with securities laws.

On January 22, 1996, Judge Lamberth again ordered Life Partners to produce key documents for the SEC's investigation. Since Life Partners had not yet complied with securities laws, His Honor also issued a preliminary order forbidding Life Partners from selling pieces (i.e., "fractional interests") of life insurance policies to investors.

> The SEC made it clear they had no intention of outlawing viatical settlements.
> Their opposition was restricted to LPI, to the way Life Partners repackaged death benefits and resold them.

Each time the court ruled against him, Pardo threatened to appeal the ruling. And so he did. And so he lost. And so he planned another appeal. And all the while Life Partners continued business. The legal system might keep Pardo's lawyers busy, but it failed to rain on his parade.

When at last the Federal hearings were concluded, Pardo added another notch to his belt. He filed suit against Leo Ornstein, the SEC attorney responsible for bringing him to court.

The NAPWA Connection

When you consider the charges against Brian Pardo, when you consider the breadth and width of fault found by the Court, it's surprising that Judge Lambert (a Reagon appointee) would show such leniency to Pardo and LPI. Perhaps His Honor viewed these charges as just another "white collar crime" — not of a serious nature.

Industry watchers have another interpretation. The Court's leniency, they say, was due to the considerable influence of The National Association for People With AIDS (NAPWA).

NAPWA was the only outside party to file a "friend at court" brief on behalf of Brian Pardo and Life Partners. NAPWA requested the Court to allow LPI to continue business without interruption. Anything else, they argued, would harm AIDS patients whose policies were in Pardo's possession. In addition, countless others would be harmed — AIDS patients who would need LPI's invaluable service in the future. NAPWA'S plea was couched to give the impression the viatical industry would come to a screeching halt without Brian Pardo.

What's behind NAPWA's support for Brian Pardo?

The first clue came months earlier, when this author sent a letter to Bill Freeman, executive director of NAPWA, requesting information about viatical settlements. Freeman responded with a message saying he had passed the letter on to Brian Pardo of

Life Partners, who would contact me. I thought this was odd, then didn't gave it a second thought. And never heard from Pardo.

As 1995 drew to a close and hearings continued at Federal court, NAPWA invited Brian Pardo to come to Los Angeles to address a national skills-building conference for 1,005 AIDS service providers. Pardo as spokesman for the viatical industry? Unacceptable to those who knew his reputation! A flurry of irate phone calls forced NAPWA to add two other speakers, thereby changing a solo performance into a panel discussion.

Several people with past or present affiliations with NAPWA explained (on conditions of anonymity) that NAPWA had a stake in the outcome of the Federal hearings, since it routinely refers clients to Pardo.

Why?

Why does NAPWA continue to refer clients to Pardo?

Answer: Pardo's philanthropy allowed NAPWA officials to "draw huge salaries and do a little charitable work on the side."

> "Mr. Pardo's philanthropy within the Gay community is well recognized."
> (quoted from LPI's Director of Corporate Communications)

Pardo with Cloak and dagger

While hearings continued at Federal court, subsidiaries of Life Partners were busy, up and down the coast of California.

In San Diego, LPI operates behind the name of National Medical Funding, supposedly a viatical funding firm. Despite

Pardo's vow never to submit to regulation, National Medical Funding applied for a license and currently solicits viatical business under license-pending status.

Need proof? The application kit sent to viators by National Medical Funding contains letters on Life Partners' letterhead, complete with Waco, Texas, address and phone, as well as National Medical's 800 number in San Diego.[34]

The kit was delivered by Airborne®. Later that same day, a prospective viator received a phone call from a man who said he was assigned by Life Partners to be "your personal caseworker."

Then there's Sterling Signatures Corporation in Walnut Creek, California, a company that markets insurance policies to investors. Following one of their radio ads on KPIX, the president and CEO of Sterling Signatures, William L. Morgan, sent out samples showing the phenomenal yields (rates of return) received on his investments in life insurance investments.

> Is it mere coincidence that one of Pardo's fronts is Sterling Signatures (Walnut Creek, CA), and the escrow/trust that LPI uses is Sterling Trust (Waco, Texas)?

Morgan also provided copies of letters signed by Brian Pardo. These letters notified Morgan about the "maturing" of several policies in which Morgan owned "fractionalized" shares." Yields were handwritten in the margins. Morgan's cover letter boasted, "I put my money where my mouth is." (sic)

Lifetime Funding, located in Aptos, describes itself as "viatical settlement specialists" and "a marketing company that manages licensees for Life Partners."[35]

Lifetime Funding targets insurance agents and financial planners, urging them to sign up clients for this high yield, low risk investment. In return, these agents/financial planners are paid a per-buyer commission. These commissions are sliced off the top of viators' settlements — another violation of California's viatical laws.[36]

This marketing packet, which used the U.S. Postal Service, displayed dual logos: Lifetime Funding and Life Partners. The kit included a letter, signed by Ken Doolittle, President of Lifetime Funding, which warned potential investors:

> ". . . many other firms have recently jumped into the market, trying to copy what we do. Several of these have committed fraud against their investors, and many more have principals with criminal backgrounds. Simply put, be careful who you deal with."[37]

This marketing packet supports nearly every allegation made by the SEC — and then some.[38] Here are a few new ones:

• **"Life Partners makes no solicitation or advertisement whatsoever to these patients or their representatives."**

What else would you call ads placed by Life Partners in gay publications? What about LPI's admission that it solicits through attorneys and insurance agents?

• **"Are death benefits taxable? Normally, yes. The gain on the transaction, when realized, is generally considered to be a taxable event."**

Wrong! Death payments normally are tax-free to

beneficiaries. But life insurance, used as an investment vehicle, is taxed . . . like other investments.

• **"One exception [to taxation of death benefits] would occur if the gain is recognized in a tax deferred qualified plan such as an IRA."**

Wrong again! IRA funds cannot be used to buy life insurance contracts. This is "a prohibited transaction" — according to Internal Revenue Code § 408(a)(3)25.

Pardo's flip-flop

Remember Pardo's comments about the insurance industry hating viatical companies? In promotional materials he poses this question: "Do Companies Object to Viatical Settlements?"

His answer is, "Normally, no . . .. Insurance companies do not care who the beneficiary is; . . . and the insurance companies have approved forms to accommodate such transfers."

Pardo's law

In the spring of 1995, Brian Pardo placed ads in Gay newspapers around the country. This time his purpose was to warn people with AIDS of the dangers of selling their life insurance to licensed viatical companies. He said:

> "Licensed firms are required by law to
> submit all pertinent information concerning
> the sale of your life insurance policy,
> including your identity, to the state
> insurance department."

Pardo added that viators' personal information would be available to state or federal agencies, such as police and the IRS.

How can this be, when not one of the states that enacted viatical regulation requires information identifying viators?

One-on-one with a Pardo Stooge

Whitaker Rehm, a caseworker at AIDS Services Foundation, asked me to check out a man who claimed to be a viatical broker. The "broker" was handling the viatical sale for a not-very-bright client. Whitaker read me the man's business card: "Insurance." That was all. Not one word about viatical settlements. Whitaker worried about his client.

These suspicions were well-grounded, although at the time no one at ASF knew that California had a viatical licensing law. Since the DOI doesn't allow dual licensing, either this "broker" wasn't licensed for insurance, or he wasn't licensed for viatical contracts. This dual licensing prohibition is based on the probability of conflicts of interest. According to the DOI,

> ". . . expertise as a licensed life agent combined with the superior financial and fiduciary position as a viatical settlement broker gives you potentially overwhelming influence over the viator who by definition has 'a catastrophic or life threatening illness or condition.' Public policy as expressed in Civil Code 1575 mandates against validating contracts where such undue influence exists."[39]

In plain English, the DOI anticipates that dual licensing

would encourage insurance agents to sell only those life policies that don't include Accelerated Death Benefits. The reason: To earn a second commission in some future year for viaticating the policy. When I first heard this, it seemed silly reasoning.

What agent would choose to spend time and effort finding insurance policies that don't include ADB? Agents are concerned with today's commissions — not some fanciful pile of dollars several years hence. On the other hand, I could envision a conflict of interest if a terminally ill client phoned for advice. The agent might steer the client toward a viatical provider instead of the insurer's ADB. But, how often might such a thing occur? I continued to scoff at the DOI's strictures against dual licensing until the day I met Ulysses (not his real name).

We arranged to meet for lunch. In preparation for the meeting, I called the DOI's Consumer Helpline to find out which license Ulysses held. It was the insurance license (life and health). There was no record that he ever applied for licensing as a viatical broker.

We lunched outdoors at Laguna Beach, within sniffing distance of the Pacific. It was a beautiful sunshiney day, but immediately spoiled by the first words uttered by Ulysses. He informed me he was gay, that he was HIV positive, that he was a client of ASF, that he routinely made the rounds of gay groups and various AIDS support groups, where he scouted for viatical clients and insurance clients — people looking for insurance that didn't require a medical exam. And he flat-out warned me that I couldn't stop him, that I would never have any influence with gay clients. He made it crystal clear that since I was not gay, I was outside the fence. If ever it came to a contest, I would automatically lose.

Later on, I realized had I not been so shocked to hear this, had my humor not been dulled by it, I could have pretended not to be "straight." How would he have known otherwise? It might have been fun to turn the tables like that . . . take away his thunder.

Continuing on without interruption, Ulysses told me he had applied for a viatical license, and was in the process of arguing with the DOI for the right to keep his insurance license. I didn't say a word about the latest list of licensees and license-pending brokers stuffed in my purse. Ulysses's name was notably absent.

I ate while Ulysses talked on and on. With an air of grandiosity, he said that he marketed policies to Life Partners. He had visited Waco, Texas, had glad handed Pardo and his coterie. The fact that Brian Pardo was not gay didn't seem significant to Ulysses.

I forgot to continue the dumb act and began to ask pointed questions. "How can you place clients with Life Partners, when they aren't licensed in California?" and, "Are you aware that LPI uses confidential medical histories as marketing materials?" and, "Are you aware that LPI consults a physician who is a shareholder and board member?"

Ulysses was so puffed up with himself, he couldn't see past his self-image. He answered every question with neat paraphrases from the mouth of Brian Pardo.

I told him I couldn't understand why he applied for a viatical license, when Pardo was so heatedly opposed to licensing.

"Because it looks good," he said.

As we parted, he handed me a bundle of rolodex® cards to distribute. The card was headed with the word, "Insurance."

I told him I wouldn't consider referring anyone to him until he represented several viatical firms.

Later, I learned that Ulysses was not an ASF client, but this no longer was significant. Ulysses had taught me what Per Larson meant when he warned:

"This is a war, and we've got to get the word out."

* * *

END NOTES

1. Names of viators are fictitious, but examples of LPI sales are assumed to be real, since they were taken from promotional materials mailed jointly by Lifetime Funding and Life Partners.

2. "SEC Sues Life Partners, Inc., Alleging Illegal Brokering of Insurance Policies," Jeffrey Taylor. The Wall Street Journal, August 26, 1995.

3. This information originally appeared in the Wall Street Journal, and was reported in "Money for Nothing, Death for Free?" Christopher Gully, Genre, January 1995.

4. "Grim Reaping," Helen Thompson, Texas Monthly, November 1992.

5. "New Industry Earning 20% on Terminally Ill," Carey Gillam. Kansas Business Journal, May 28-June 3, 1993.

6. Thompson, Ibid.
Taylor, Ibid.
"Pre-Death Cash: A Business Grows," Michael Quint. The New York Times, November 14, 1994.
"Judge Rules Viatical Company Must Comply with Securities Laws," Jose Zuniga. The Washington Blade, August 4, 1995.

"Court Says Life Partners Broke Securities Laws," Michael Quint. The New York Times, September 1, 1995.
"Judge Curbs Insurance Firms 'Viatical' Deals," Albert B. Crenshaw. The Washington Post, January 24, 1996.

7. "A Discourse on Viatical Settlements," M.L. Higgins. California Broker, December 1995.

8. As described by journalist Pamela Sherrid in U.S. News & World Report, August 21, 1995.

9. Quint, Ibid.

10. Higgins, Ibid.

11. "Rules for Companies that Buy Life Policies," Nick Ravo, The New York Times, June 11, 1994.

12. "Enriching the Final Days," Pamela Sherrid, U.S. News & World Report, August 21, 1995.

13. Ibid.

14. "Money for Nothing, Death for Free?" Christopher Gully, Genre, January 1995.

15. Quint, November 14, 1994, Ibid.

16. Higgins, Ibid.

17. Rick Perry of Life Today has an endless number of similar stories.

18. Phone interviews with Meir Eliav (Legacy Benefits), and Alan Perper and Bradley Rutter (Dignity Partners).

19. Jet, September 7, 1992.

20. Phone interview with Tom Day.

21. "Fed Court Regulates Viaticals," Rob Roehr, The Texas Triangle, September 1995.

22. "Merchants of Death Benefits Get New Rules," Susan Harrigan. New York Newsday, August 4, 1994.

23. "Money for Nothing, Death for Free?" Christopher Guly, Genre, January 1995.

24. The source, Higgins's article in the December 1995 issue of California Broker, was either confirmed or elaborated upon by industry leaders. On instructions from her attorney, Ms. Ayoob refused to comment about Pardo's lawsuit.

25. Taylor, Ibid.

26. Jet. NASA brought these charges against another firm, as well: National Insurance Marketing, Inc. of Panama City, Florida.

27. Taylor, Ibid.

28. "Let the Seller Beware," Jose Zuniga, The Washington Blade, August 4, 1995. Also see Sherrid's article in U.S. News & World Report.

29. Zuniga's primary reference was Securities Regulation and Law Report, a publication of the private reporting firm, The Bureau of National Affairs.

30. Gully, Ibid.

31. Zuniga, Ibid.

32. "Life Partners Told to Transfer Its Life Policies," Amy J. Schatz. The Wall Street Journal, September 1, 1995.

33. Schatz, Ibid.

34. The phone number for Life Partners is 800-700-7334.

35. The phone number for Lifetime Funding is 800-347-2290.

36. As described in an ad placed in California Broker, December, 1995 (on the same page as Higgins' tribute to Brian Pardo), and also in the marketing kit distributed jointly by Lifetime Funding and Life Partners, Inc.

37. A copy of Doolittle's letter, dated September 26, 1995, is in the author's possession.

38. Marketing materials distributed through the U.S. postal service (September, 1995).

39. Excerpt from a California Department of Insurance letter to Nancy Cane of Benefit Advocates, March 30, 1995.

CHAPTER 7

Your Life Insurance

The focus here is narrow: aspects of life insurance that effect viatical settlements and Accelerated Death Benefits; and, how to get insurance after a diagnosis is made.

Is it better to cash out a policy, or take a loan?[1]

When you cash out your insurance, you surrender the policy. This means all protection is lost. But if you take a loan, you'll get the same amount of money and continue to be insured, in exchange for paying loan interest.

What if I can't afford to pay loan interest?

Take the loan, then ask the insurer about nonforfeiture options.

What are nonforfeiture options?

Instead of surrendering the policy, you can use the surrender value (the cash within the policy) to buy a reduced amount of paid up insurance.

Reduced paid insurance gives you the exact same type of policy, but with a smaller death benefit. Since the policy will be paid up, you'll never have to pay premiums.

If you have Universal or Variable Life, the same result can be accomplished by reducing the face amount to a level that can be supported by the cash value indefinitely — with no further premium payments.

Is there a downside to reduced paid up insurance?

Not with Universal or Variable Life. But if you exchange whole life for reduced paid-up insurance, this exchange will terminate all riders and supplementary benefits (such as riders for disability and accidental death).

If you don't want less insurance, you could exchange the cash value in the original policy for extended term insurance. Since term insurance is cheaper, you'll have the same face amount as with the original whole life/cash value policy.

What is the advantage to extended term insurance?

No further premiums are required. The cash value of the original policy is used to pay all future premiums.

Is there a downside to extended term insurance?[2]

You will be insured for the same amount as the cash value policy (without further premium payments), but extended term lasts only until the cash value is used up. When that happens, the insurance expires. However, if you have a shortened life expectancy, refer to the insurer's proposal to calculate whether the policy will stay in force past that estimate.

Are these types of policies accepted for viatical settlements?

Nearly any type of insurance can be sold — if there are no serious problems with the policy.

What kind of insurance problems effect viatical settlements?

First, underwriters examine your policy and the annual statement, then send a questionnaire to the insurer for confirmation of this information. This is what they look for:

- *Age*. The policy must be older than two years.
- *Lapses and reinstatements*. If you didn't pay the premium, and your policy entered the grace period — then lapsed — then was reinstated when you paid the overdue premiums, you may have a problem. Reinstatements usually trigger a new two year incontestability period.
- *Policy holder* (a.k.a. policy owner). Viatical providers prefer the insured to be owner, since this simplifies transfer of ownership. Problems are rare when the owner is an insured's family member, friend, or life insurance trust. But there may be problems if the policy is part of a group or association trust. Details about converting employee group or association group insurance are in Chapter 1.

> "Because of the problems with conversion, we can't advise clients to convert. We'll look into it, tell the client what we found out, and let the client make the decision about conversion. Up to this point we cannot say that we'll buy it."
> — Brian Klein (Neuma)

- *Absolute Assignment*. The Absolute Assignment form is used to transfer complete ownership to another party. With group policies, the question is, "Does the master contract allow you to transfer ownership?"

As recently as twenty years ago there were laws in most states that prevented group term from being assigned to another owner. But in the past two decades nearly all states eliminated this prohibition, and many (not all) insurers modified their contracts to permit assignment.

Note: Some insurers allow you to assign group policies as a gift — but not for value (money), and some don't allow the policy to be assigned to a corporation.

If the Benefit Handbook describes the policy as not assignable, don't give up. Most insurers will waive this prohibition upon request.

- *Beneficiaries*. Two key issues:

Do you want to keep some benefits for an irrevocable beneficiary? *Irrevocable* means unchangeable, permanent. Some viatical providers won't be bothered with irrevocable beneficiaries. If you decide to keep some benefits for an irrevocable beneficiary, you can do so but it will limit your choices of viatical providers. (See the grid in the Appendix.)

> "Sixty percent of our business is group, and about 90% of the groups that I see are doable in one fashion or another."
> — Rick Perry (Life Today)

Some employee group policies don't allow the insured to name a beneficiary who isn't a family member. This is why such policies couldn't be sold — until recently. Now it is possible, says Rick Perry (Life Today).

According to Perry, the legal departments of many leading insurers make all sorts of exceptions that benefit terminally ill insureds. When there's a conversion problem, it's usually due to the employer, or a small insurer that never heard of viatical settlements — and rarely the large, well-known insurers.

- *Stability*. Group insurance, again. Small employer and association groups often are not stable. They may cancel the master contract, leaving you without insurance. Or they may switch to another insurance carrier. Due to this added risk, group insurance is discounted 5 to 7 percent.
- *Conversion conditions*. Upon conversion, some insurers reinstate the two year incontestability period. The effect is to treat the conversion policy as if it were a new policy; you won't be able to sell it for two years. To find out if this applies to you, check your employee Benefit Handbook, or phone the agent who sold the plan to the group.

The majority of problems occur when insureds didn't participate in the group plan for the full five years specified in the contract. Then the master contract may not give you the right to convert, or may greatly reduce the amount of insurance you can convert. See Chapter 1 for details.

> "For the most part, we can work on changing the conversion cap. For example, when a policy for $100,000 converts to $2,000. Usually it's the employer, not the insurance company, who won't cooperate."
> — Kevin Kurth (Access)

If your group had less than twenty employees, there may be no provision for continuation of coverage (or conversion) when employment ends.[3]

- *Face value*: Do death benefits decrease? Mortgage insurance has decreasing face values. As the loan is paid off, the death benefit reduces. Until last year, no provider would touch decreasing term. Now it is saleable — but you'll have to ask providers if they accept this type policy. For an example of how a viatical settlement is calculated, see *True Stories* (below).
- *Face value*: Will it increase? This is an asset for which you should be paid extra. One way death benefits may increase is through a rider known as *Accidental Death and Dismemberment* (AD&D).[4] Reserve the right to keep AD&D benefits for your beneficiaries.

Another way to increase face values is through Guaranteed Insurability Options. Details are in Chapters 1 and 3.

- *Premium waiver*. For a small extra charge, the premium waiver can be added (as a rider) to most individual policies. The waiver usually is included with group term policies, but called, *extended death benefits*.

The waiver can be activated when an insured has been totally disabled for six months or longer. The rider "excuses" payment of premiums for the duration of disability. There's an added benefit with group term: You will continue to be insured, even if the master contract is terminated.

Yet another advantage to premium waivers, if you decide to sell your insurance: the settlement will be higher — since premiums won't have to be paid.

- *Increasing premiums*. Increasing premiums are common to term insurance — both individual and group term. If your policy is *Annually Renewable Term* (ART), also called *Yearly Renewable Term* (YRT), you're insured for one year at a time, but have a guaranteed right to renew the insurance at the end of each twelve month period. Each time you renew, the cost increases.

Five Year and Ten Year Term work in a similar fashion: Premiums are level for that period, then increase at renewal. It's this renewal rate that interests viatical providers. These rates — two columns of numbers — usually are found on the second or third page of the policy. The first column is the standard (maximum) rate. To qualify for the lower, re-entry rate, you must provide *evidence of insurability*.

> Increasing premiums lower your settlement — unless you have a premium waiver.

- *Government insurance* (SGLI, VGLI, and FEGLI)

Servicemen's/women's Group Life Insurance (SGLI) is sponsored by the federal government and issued by government-approved commercial life insurers. These policies provide $35,000 of group term, but cannot be assigned. Thus, if you wish to sell your insurance, you must convert to an individual policy.

The conversion policy is five-year nonrenewable term, known as Veteran's Group Life Insurance (VGLI). When the VGLI has been in force for five years, you can convert to an individual cash value policy. Similar to VGLI, this cash value policy is issued by one of a list of approved commercial life insurers. Most important, it's issued at standard rates — regardless of health — and for the same face amount as SGLI. Since this individual policy can be assigned, it can be sold.

Federal Employees Group Life Insurance (FEGLI) is group term insurance provided to all government employees, including those who are in service. Unlike SGLI and VGLI, these policies are issued by a pool of insurance companies. When your Federal employment ends, these approved carriers are allowed to offer a conversion option to individual insurance.

FEGLI policies provide additional insurance called, "Extra Benefit," to insureds who are terminally ill and under age forty-five. If the insured is age 35 or younger, this Extra Benefit doubles the amount of insurance.

> "Military policies (SGLI or VGLI) cannot be assigned nor given irrevocable beneficiaries. The insured must stay in the VGLI for a minimum of 5 years. Then the policy can be continued or converted to individual insurance. If a person is considering a viatical, it is better to convert."
> — Carl Holland (Lifetime Options)

It used to be that FEGLI policies had to be coverted to private insurance before they could be sold. In the summer of 1994, the rules changed. Now you can assign all death benefits, supplemental as well as basic. Now it's your choice, if you want to sell to a viatical provider.

But you might not choose to. FEGLI policies now offer Accelerated Death Benefits. This rider was added to FEGLI policies in 1995. By taking the ADB on a policy worth $100,000, you would lose $4,900 — as opposed to a loss of $20,000 (possibly more) through a viatical settlement. And the ADB is faster and easier.

You know what they say about something that sounds too good to be true? And there are a few flies in the ointment:

- Accelerated Death Benefits are not payable until your life expectancy is nine months or less.

- The ADB rider applies only to basic coverage. This means, if you use the ADB, you lose (forever) the supplemental insurance. But if you convert, you can keep the added benefits, and can sell this larger amount to a viatical provider.
- Taxes: Until the tax-free bill is implemented, Accelerated Death Benefits from FEGLI will continue to be reported to IRS. You'll be sent a 1099-R for these Accelerated Death Benefits, and owe taxes on the amount.

Worse news: If you take ADB while you're collecting Social Security benefits, you may be liable for an additional tax on a portion of the Social Security (see Chapter 8, *Tax Tips*).

True Stories

Dennis: How do viatical providers calculate the face amount on decreasing term insurance?

There are two calculations — death benefits, and life expectancy. Dennis owned a decreasing term policy with an original face amount of $92,000. When he decided to viaticate, the face amount had decreased by nearly twenty thousand.

Dennis sent applications to six viatical providers. Within three weeks he had three settlement offers. Ten nail-biting days later, two more offers came in (the sixth viatical provider never responded). The last two offers turned out to be the highest bids (and identical). Dennis sent them back to slug it out. This is what happened:

Each viatical firm calculated life expectancy, then figured what the policy would be worth at a future time, based on their estimate of Dennis' life expectancy. Each provider then offered a percentage that appeared to safeguard their risk. Of the five bids, the lowest were in the range of 69 - 70 percent (of the face amount, which was $71,000 and $72,000). The highest bids (from the two viatical firms who responded last) were 80 percent of $72,883 — a difference of nearly ten thousand dollars!

Sheryl: Is it possible to get a group term policy converted after the conversion cutoff date? The conversion cutoff date was two days ago.

This depends on the insurer. In this case, the insurer was John Hancock. I advised Sheryl to send the papers ASAP. Since it was the start of a week-end, the papers would arrive a week late. Yet, it was possible that John Hancock wouldn't fuss.

Well, good ole John Hancock came through — like the troopers I thought they were. The policy was issued without a peep — and with the same issue date as the original employer group term. This put the new policy past the incontestability period. Next, Sheryl applied for the Accelerated Death Benefit rider. As soon as the rider was added to her policy, she applied for the benefit. One month later the money was nestled in her bank account.

Ben: My insurer won't make good on its promise. When I changed jobs seven years ago, I converted from group term to an individual policy. Since then, I paid the premiums, took a loan from cash value, paid loan interest. Now that I'm disabled, I dug out this letter from the insurer:

> "You probably share one anxiety that many people tell us they have today: the possibility of terminal illness or prolonged nursing care that poses a financial threat. The New England, which has a long tradition of concern for its policyholders, is pleased to respond to this critical and timely issue with a new Accelerated

> Benefits Rider. This rider enables benefits to be paid before death if the insured becomes terminally ill. The New England is one of the few insurers to provide this benefit which will be reflected in the revisions being made on existing policies."

The letter asks and answers questions about the new rider. Among these: the rider would be added to existing insurance "at the time you are ready to file a claim." Another: the benefit could be exercised "when the insured policyholder has a medical condition that is expected to result in death within six months as certified by a licensed medical doctor." At the bottom of the letter, in tiny print, there was a warning: "Eligibility depends on state restrictions and policy type and will be determined at the time of claim."

Ben phoned The New England and asked to have the ADB rider added to his policy. He was told the rider was not available for Omega conversion policies, which was the type Ben had owned for seven years.

> The Omega was specifically designed for conversion policies — for insureds who are health risks.

It was at this point that I entered the picture, speaking first with a vice president, then with a head underwriter who helped design this rider. I reminded them of the two million dollar multi-media campaign recently launched by the insurance industry to remind people of the value of death benefits. Among other things, I tossed Brian Pardo's words at them and asked,

Did they want to prove Pardo right about the insurance industry?

The Veep said he might be able to do something. It was Friday afternoon; he promised to phone me on Monday.

Instead of the Veep, it was the head underwriter who phoned. When she said nothing could be done, I read her the blurb from the New England's letter: "The New England is one of the few insurers to provide this benefit which will be reflected in the revisions being made on existing policies."

"There never was any intention to add the ADB rider to existing policies," she said. "We add it to new issues, but not to in-force insurance."

Finally I asked, "How about a 1035 exchange?" She gasped, recovered from the shock, and said she would look into it.

I had hoped The New England would come up with the idea without my help. Then I could have acted surprised . . . pleased — and praised them mightily. The 1035 exchange — the old policy exchanged for a new one — would give Ben the exact same death benefit, but it would allow him to have the Accelerated Death Benefits rider.

"If the legal department approves this," I added, "it must be with the original issue day." This was important. The alternative — today's date — would renew the incontestability period, which would require Ben to wait two years before he could get Accelerated Death Benefits.

The head underwriter was diligent: She phoned each day throughout the week, even when she had no progress to report. She admitted that the problem was the legal department — they were fearful of setting a precedent.

"To date," she said, "we've turned down thirty requests for ADB."

At last the decision came down. The 1035 exchange was

approved — but with a current date.

Fortunately, Ben had an alternative. It wasn't as fast, as simple, or as much money as the insurer's ADB. Ben knew he would lose at least 20 percent of the face value. But it could have been worse. He could have been without an alternative.

Two months later Ben received a viatical settlement — 70 percent of the death benefit.

Peter: What happens when an insured slips through the cracks?

Two years earlier, before being discharged from a VA hospital, Peter decided to convert his FEGLI policy to individual ownership. He gave the conversion papers to an employee, and requested they be turned in at the proper office.

When the doctor gave him the news that he had a six month life expectancy, Peter decided to viaticate his insurance. He sent an application to a funding firm, which is how he learned that no conversion had taken place. Peter hadn't been insured for the past two years.

After being rejected by the funding firm, Peter turned to a broker recommended by a friend. Carole Fiedler (Fiedler Financial) called the Office of Policy & Management in Washington, D.C. (numerous times), and finally accomplished what seemed impossible: The right to convert was offered anew to Peter. Now that he had that right, Fiedler located a life insurance agent in the Seattle area who could handle the conversion. Through agent Randy Kim, Peter paid 24 months of back premiums and the policy was converted. The new insurer was John Hancock, and the new policy was successfully viaticated.

Karen: Is it possible to get insurance after diagnosis?

This same question was asked several years ago by a friend who is a social worker at a leading east coast hospital. She asked on behalf of a patient who had received a heart-lung transplant and wanted to spare his family the burden of final expenses. Then, as now, there was a special type of insurance for people with serious health conditions. It's known as guaranteed issue, or graded life.

Guaranteed issue means applicants don't have to answer health questions or take a medical exam.

Graded life, or graded death benefit pays less if death occurs from natural causes (e.g., illness) during the early years of the policy. For example, full death benefits are paid after the policy has been in force for two, three, or four years — the number of years depends on the insurer's contract. However, if death occurs from an accident, the full death benefit is paid immediately.

On a three year contract, if the insured dies of natural causes in the first policy year, beneficiaries receive all premiums that were paid, plus interest (usually at 10 percent). After year one, one-third of the death benefit is paid. After year two, two-thirds of the death benefit is paid. After year three, the full amount is paid.

Is there a downside to guaranteed issue life?

There are several. Death benefits are limited — sometimes as low as $5,000 and rarely more than $50,000, although one or two insurers do issue amounts in the six figures.

If you can afford to do this, buy several small policies (no questions are asked about other insurance).

Another flaw: These policies are not available with disability waiver of premium.

But the greatest problem may be states that don't allow these policies to be sold to people under 50 years of age (e.g., New York). If the state permits it, some insurers won't sell these policies to people under 50 years. If you travel to a state that allows these policies at any age, some insurers won't accept applications signed by a nonresident.

Heed the words of David Peterson, founder of Affording Care. Peterson warns against jeopardizing an out of state application by handling it solely through the mail. Additionally, he advises insureds to provide executors with documentation to prove you were in the other state at the time you applied.

"Store copies of your travel documents ('air or train fare, hotel bills, credit card chits') in your policy file."[5]

What do these policies cost?

As you might have guessed, the cost for these policies is far greater than standard issue. The annual cost for a person age 30 is $20 per thousand. By contrast, medically underwritten permanent life costs $9 per thousand; term life costs $2 per thousand.

Premiums are level, meaning, they don't increase or decrease. As with all life insurance, cost is calculated in multiples of a thousand.

Guaranteed issue is a good choice for critically ill people who have family to protect. Since these policies pay between 8 and 12 percent interest on premiums, if you die during the first year, the interest is added to the death benefit and paid tax-free to your heirs.

Can guaranteed life policies be exchanged for a viatical settlement?

Yes, once the policy is past the three-year graded benefit period.

* * *

END NOTES

1. This question refers only to whole life (permanent) insurance, since term insurance doesn't have cash values.

2. Employee Benefits, Burton T. Beam, Jr. and John J. McFadden. Richard D. Irwin, Inc., Ill., 1985.

3. The January/February 1993 issued of "Affording Care Bulletin" includes an excellent article by Brent Nance, CLU, RHU about continuation insurance mandated by The Consolidated Omnibus Budget Reconciliation Act of 1986 (COBRA). Copies are available from Affording Care at (212) 262-9449.

4. This rider pays additional death benefits when death is due to accident, or the insured suffers loss of limbs.

5. David told this to me by phone, but full details are in the Affording Care Bulletin, March/April 1993, "Life Insurance — No Questions Asked," by David Peterson.

Chapter 8

Tax Tips

This chapter is primarily intended for your advisors, but read the topics that apply to you. If you find a tax tip that fits your situation, it may save you several hundred dollars. At the least, you'll have questions to ask your financial advisors, and you'll be better able to understand their answers.

How are viatical settlements taxed?

For Federal taxes purposes, viatical settlements are taxed exactly the same as Accelerated Death Benefits — as ordinary income. And the news gets worse. If the lump sum payment is large enough, your Social Security benefits will become taxable. This is what happened to Harry.

When Harry's sole source of income was Social Security, he

wasn't required to file a tax return. Last year he took an Accelerated Death Benefit from his FEGLI policy. The following January he found Form 1099R in his mailbox. Now he knew that his $30,000 ADB had been reported to IRS. This meant that he was required to file a tax return.

Harry filed as a single person, and used the Standard Deduction. His tax debt was $3,566 — 12 percent of the ADB.

But the ADB also made Harry's Social Security taxable. This increased his tax liability to a grand total of $6,699 — a loss of 22 percent of the Accelerated Death Benefit.

Do viatical providers send out Form 1099R?

Since there's no reporting requirement for viatical providers, they won't send you Form 1099R. Nor is there a requirement for insurers to report Accelerated Death Benefits — and they don't. But you will get Form 1099R, if your ADB comes from government insurance.

> Private insurers are required to report only the contractual interest paid on death claims. This is the amount earned on insurance proceeds from date of death to date of payment.

Keep in mind, even though you may not receive Form 1099R, it doesn't mean you're home free. Under current law, all viators are required to file a tax return and report these payments. This requirement will be waived, when Congress finally gets its act together and passes a budget — but only for people whose life expectancies are two years or less.

Tax-free status won't apply to people with life expectancies longer than two years.

What if a viator with a two year life expectancy lives longer?

Estimation of life expectancy is not an exact science — which is one reason why countless numbers of people outlive their doctor's prognosis. In other words, it's no crime to outlive your life expectancy. So, go ahead — do it.

Actually, proposed regulations take this uncertainty into account. Tax-free status will apply if the insured has an "illness or physical condition that, despite appropriate medical care, is reasonably expected to result in death" within that 24 month period.[1]

If I have a three year life expectancy, will my payment be taxed?

According to the wording of the bill: yes.

Why is the government willing to make these benefits tax-free?

Because there is a financial advantage to the government. Tax-free status will encourage more insureds to use their life insurance proceeds, and this will keep them off government benefits for a longer period.

And there are other reasons:

- Currently, viatical settlements are taxed twice — once to the seller (the viator) and a second time to the buyer (the investor).
- When these benefits are tax-free to insureds, the

government will continue to tax the gain to investors.

- When death benefits are paid in the traditional manner — after death — the government doesn't get a plug nickel. This is why it pays handsomely for the government to encourage the use of pre-death benefits from life insurance.

Will benefits received earlier this year be "grandfathered?"

It appears unlikely that tax-free status will be retroactive ("grandfathered"). Alan Perper (Dignity Partners) was one of the viatical industry leaders who testified before Congress on behalf of this bill. Perper believes the effective date of the bill will be January 1, 1997 — with no provision to grandfather benefits paid in 1996.

> Jack decided to file a tax return and pay the tax on his viatical settlement. He hoped that the new medical protocol he recently began would give him a normal life span. If that happened, he didn't want his future marred by IRS problems.

What about state income taxes?

Where there is a state income tax, if the state has enacted viatical regulation, these benefits are exempt from state taxes. Residents of New York or California will have to make an adjustment on the state tax return. Even if you owe no state tax, you'll have to file, but you'll subtract any "living benefits" and/or Social Security that were federally taxed.

What portion of insurance benefits is taxable?

It varies. If premiums were paid entirely by an employer, the entire benefit is taxable. If you paid all premiums out of pocket, you'll be taxed on the "adjusted" basis. Adjusted basis means what it cost you, less benefits you already received (e.g., dividends). To calculate the gain, add all premiums paid for basic insurance (not for riders) + taxable dividends + accrued interest + outstanding loans. Subtract this sum from the viatical settlement (or Accelerated Death Benefit). The difference is your gain.

If dividends were used to buy additional insurance, are they treated as premiums?

There are two types of dividends: One is taxable, and the other is not. But either type, if used to buy more insurance, can be considered premiums.

Must I pay estimated taxes on the ADB or viaticum?

No — if you had no tax liability in the previous year (a 12 month period), and were a U.S. citizen or resident for the entire year.

No — if you were working at the time you received these benefits, and you paid taxes equal to 100 percent of the previous year's taxes.

Yes — if neither of these situations apply, you may be required to pay estimated taxes. Since tax law is complex (actually tax "whim" rather than tax law), and since it's ever-changing, check with a tax advisor before determining what course to take.

Medical expenses ate up the ADB; nothing is left to pay taxes.

If you owe taxes but are unable to pay, do the following:

- File the tax return, taking care to use all the deductions to which you are entitled.

- Attach a Supplementary Schedule in which you detail your medical expenses.

- Ask your doctor to sign Schedule R. Attach this schedule to your tax return.

- Include the financial forms required to submit an Offer in Compromise. These forms will substantiate there is nothing for IRS to collect.

> Schedule R is intended for disabled people who qualify for a credit. But you can use it as evidence of a disability that impairs your ability to pay taxes, or as evidence that penalties should be waived.

- You may want to include a written statement explaining your special circumstances. Special circumstances may be similar to that of Jack, age 59, who was laid off during his wife's final bout with cancer. While Jack sought employment, his wife's illness exhausted their health insurance, ate up their savings, and finally cost them their home. IRS needs to be informed of these circumstances, in order to act appropriately.

What types of expenses are overlooked?

Frequently overlooked expenses include:

- Mortgage interest, not only for houses and condos, but stationary or mobile trailers
- Real estate and other property taxes
- Contributions to charity. This includes cash and tangible items, and travel expenses related to volunteer work
- Medical expenses. Most people think of sickness-related expenses, but you can deduct fees for eye exams, dental visits, counseling, chiropractic care, acupuncture, etc.
- Phone charges: Is your physician out of the toll-free dialing area? Phone charges are a legitimate deduction.
- Premiums for medical, dental, hospital insurance
- Fees for travel and parking — air, car, or bus — and costs for a driver, when necessary. Don't forget trips to and from the pharmacy
- Overnight travel expense (hotel and food) related to health care, including expenses for a traveling companion
- Prescription items, both medical and miscellaneous, such as eyeglasses

> Most people are unaware of all the deductions available to them. Many seriously ill people overlook medical expenses that, when bunched together, may tip the scales in your favor.

- Nonprescription items prescribed for health reasons (e.g., bottled water, crutches, vitamins, food supplements)

If you're on a special diet, you may deduct only the

difference between the ordinary cost of food and the additional cost of the special diet

- In home health care (e.g., supplies, home health aide)

If you are legally blind, you will qualify for an extra exemption on your tax return.

Must I file a tax return if I don't owe taxes?

No, but you should — if you're due a refund. Refunds are not sent automatically. You may be due a refund, if your employer withheld taxes from your earnings. Or you may be due a refund in the form of a credit. You may qualify for Earned Income Credit — even if you didn't pay any tax, and owe no tax.

Doesn't Earned Income Credit apply only to working parents?

It did, but no longer. Beginning with tax year 1994, Earned Income Credit was extended to all low wage earners — as an incentive to accept work even if the work paid minimum wage. As of tax year 1995, an individual earner who had no dependent children could qualify for EIC if the total of all taxable and nontaxable income was less than $9,230.

"A lot of people are paper poor for the purposes of EIC," said Thomas McCormack, the foremost specialist in government benefits.[2] "Most of their income may not be taxable for AGI (Adjusted Gross Income) purposes. Yet they qualify for EIC, which can generate a substantial refund."

What about an adult child who returns home for his final illness?

This is an area of tax law not commonly known to most tax

practitioners. In this situation, if the parent of an adult disabled child has earnings, the parent may qualify for Earned Income Credit — regardless of the age of the child.

Among the criteria to qualify an adult child:

- Disability. The child was permanently and totally disabled at any time during the tax year.[3]

- Residency. The child must have lived with the parent for a part of the year. The residency test is satisfied if the child was absent from the parent's home due to a special circumstance, such as hospitalization, or if the child died during the year.

> According to McCormack: "A disabled child with an income of $50,000 returns to Mom to die. Most of Mom's income is from early retirement Social Security — $10,000. But she also has a small amount of earnings from a part time job as school crossing guard. Mom does EIC on the forty year old kiddy, and generates a refund of $3,000. And she does not have to declare the child's income on her return."

Is it possible to take a domestic partner as dependent?

Yes — if all five dependency tests are met.[4] These tests are:

- Member of household
- Citizenship
- Gross Income
- Support
- Joint Return

What is the member of household test?

To qualify as your dependent, this person must have lived in your home as a family member for the entire year.[5] This requirement is flexible: it allows for temporary absences due to special circumstances of either party. Special circumstances may be school, hospitalization, or placement in a nursing home for an indefinite time, in order to receive constant medical care. Additionally, if the person meets all requirements but dies during the year, the residency test is satisfied and that person can be considered a dependent.

What is the citizenship test?

This is very broad. It embraces not only those who are U.S. citizens or residents, but also anyone who is a resident of Canada or Mexico for some part of the calendar year. No, this is not a mistake: U.S. citizenship is not required.

> Gross income doesn't include non-taxable Social Security benefits.

What is the gross income test?

The general rule is that you can take the dependency exemption if your non-relative's gross income was no greater than the exemption amount ($2,500 for 1995).

For this purpose, don't count as gross income any tax-exempt funds, such as welfare or nontaxable social security benefits.

With this single exception, gross income includes all income, both taxable (e.g., earnings, federally taxed unemployment compensation), and non-taxable (e.g., military housing and subsistence, and contributions to 401[K] plans).

What is the support test?

In general, to claim a non-relative as your dependent, you must provide more than half that person's total support during the calendar year. But there are exceptions.

First, total support is not the same as gross income. Unlike gross income, support includes social security. Thus, if the person received and *used* Social Security payments or welfare benefits for support, these items must be included in the support test. But if your dependent didn't use this income for living expenses (he or she blew it all at Las Vegas), you can take the dependency exemption.

> Support includes food, shelter, clothing, medical and dental care, and may include a car and furniture, if they are for that person's own use or benefit. Support isn't limited to necessities. It may include recreation, gifts, vacations.

In some situations, if you provided no more than 10 percent support, you may take the dependency exemption. If others (family members or friends) paid the balance — to a total of 51 percent of expenses — and they agree, you can take the dependency exemption.

To calculate the amount of support you provided, compare the amount you contributed with the total amount of support that person received from all sources — and actually used for support.

What is the joint return test?

If the dependent files a joint return with a spouse, you are not allowed the dependency exemption.

> A non-relative may qualify as your dependent, but doesn't qualify you as Head of Household.

How are premature withdrawals of an IRA taxed?

The general rule is that money that isn't taxed going in will be taxed going out. If your IRA was fully deductible when you invested, it will be fully taxable when you withdraw it — both on the federal and state levels. The opposite is true if the IRA was non-deductible going in: You won't be taxed on withdrawals of *principal* (the amount you invested). But interest earned is taxable.

This gets far more complicated if you have both taxable and non-taxable contributions. In fact, this can be a major headache. Don't try to figure it out yourself.

If you're under age 59½ when you withdraw funds from an IRA or any other qualified retirement trust (QRT), you may also be charged penalties. This is an additional tax: on the federal level an added 10 percent, and another 2½ percent from California's Franchise Tax Board.

But if you time it right, these penalties will be waived — saving you hundreds, possibly thousands of dollars.

What is the best time to cash out an IRA?

There are two timing issues: income tax and penalties charged in addition to this tax.

Penalties for premature withdrawals are waived if medical expenses are equal to the amount of premature withdrawal. They also are waived if your doctor considers you unable to work due to total and/or permanent disability. The lesson to be learned from this: don't withdraw funds from your IRA until your circumstances dovetail with one of these rules.

The other timing issue may determine the size of the premature withdrawal, as well as *when* you take this action. The reason is that the size of the withdrawal may cause your Social Security benefits to be taxed. Knowing this, you can avoid additional taxes by cashing out the retirement plan before you apply for Social Security disability. Then you will avoid the tax on Social Security benefits.

However, if you already are receiving Social Security disability and decide to take a premature withdrawal, don't cash out the entire fund. Take only what you need now, and leave the rest in a liquid IRA, such as a money market mutual fund.

> Premature withdrawals from an IRA (or other Qualified Retirement Trusts) can cost you plenty — unless you time it exactly right. The cost: hefty penalties in addition to income tax.

Are other QRT plans taxed the same as IRAs?

In general, the same rules apply to premature withdrawals from other QRT, such as annuities, 401(K), Keogh, SEPP, and various employer pension plans. The major difference is employer pension plans automatically deduct 20 percent for taxes, before sending you the proceeds. You'll have to file a tax return to get a refund of those funds.

How do viatical settlements affect Social Security benefits?

Since there are two types of Social Security benefits, there are two answers. Your right to Social Security Disability won't be impaired by other income, but other income can cause the benefits to be taxable — as much as 85 percent of the benefit may be taxed. Whether benefits are taxable, as well as what percentage is taxed, depend on total income for your filing status (as determined by a complicated IRS formula).[6]

The opposite is true of Supplemental Security Income. Since SSI is "means-based," it won't become taxable but it may be forfeited by a substantial increase in income.[7]

What should I do about a Social Security overpayment?

You're required to repay it. In most situations the Social Security Administration subtracts the overpayment from current benefits. In other words, if you received an overpayment last year, that amount will be deducted from this year's benefits.

Does the overpayment affect the tax on viatical settlements?

No. And don't include the overpayment, when you sit down to calculate whether a viaticum will cause your Social Security benefits to be taxable. Use only the Social Security benefits paid to you for the current year.

What should I do about a lump sum Social Security payment that was due last year but paid this year?

If you expect a lump sum payment from Social Security, don't position yourself for a higher tax by getting a lump sum payment for your life insurance. Hold off for another year before selling your policy or applying for ADB.

As for the payment itself, you're not required to file an amended return for the earlier year. That's the easy part. Now for the hard stuff:

- First, treat the lump sum as if it were paid in the earlier year. Run numbers to see if those benefits would have been taxable, if paid in the earlier year. If the answer is no, simply subtract the lump sum from this year's calculations.

- If the answer is yes — if it would have been taxable in the previous year — add the taxable portion to this year's amount and pay tax on the total.

Is it possible to leave the balance of my viatical settlement to my partner without causing him to lose means-based benefits?

This is similar to a problem solved years ago by estate planners — for parents of disabled adult children. Then, as now, the issue was entitlements: How to leave money to a disabled person, without imperilling their government subsistence benefits.[8]

The key to protecting public assistance is to isolate and earmark the inheritance so that it can't be used for basic living expenses or for medical care. The way to isolate the funds is to put them into a locked box — a special drawer that opens only for "Special Needs."

Special needs may be vacations, or luxury items (like TV or CD players), or special foods, such as organically-grown fruits and vegetables. Special needs funds can't be used for ordinary living expenses, and can't buy anything that will belong to the disabled adult. (The trust will own the TV or CD player.)

This leads us to the third essential rule: These funds must be for the temporary use of the disabled person. A "remainder" beneficiary must be named — someone who will eventually get possession of the trust funds and property purchased with these funds.

This is the essence of a Living Irrevocable Special Needs Trust. A living trust is one that you (as grantor) set up during your lifetime. Irrevocable means: You can't change your mind and cancel. (It's possible to change your mind by not funding the trust, but that's another story.)

Special Needs Trusts may be called Supplementary Trusts, or Discretionary Trusts. This type trust manages funds used only for special needs, and owns any tangible items purchased for the use of the disabled, temporary beneficiary.

To familiarize yourself with the requirements of such a trust, see of one the excellent books published by Nolo Press and available at your local library.[9] Read and learn for one purpose, and one purpose only: to gain understanding. Don't attempt to use a book or computer program to set up your own trust. Since this is an extremely complicated area of law, if you attempt to forego the help of a competent attorney, you're likely to end up knee-deep in manure.

Yes, yes, I know — an attorney means legal fees. But the alternative is a trust pock-marked with flaws. But you want a trust that's done properly, so that it will solve two big problems:

- Keep your estate out of probate, and
- Protect your partner's means-based benefits

Probate can tie up your estate for several years, and put these funds out of your partner's reach. On the other hand, by avoiding probate you not only save time, but also the huge costs of Probate — costs far greater than attorney fees for designing the trust. The key to keeping down legal costs is to find the right attorney.[10]

> Watch out for trusts advertised at $395. Ask what the price includes. "Do you get separate duplicate copies of everything, or is that an extra fee? Is there an extra fee for notary services? With those $350 ads, everything's billed separately."
> — David McDowell, Esq.

How would a Special Needs Trust work for me?

This is a tricky area. Trust laws are continuously reviewed, changed, narrowed. This makes it harder and harder to design a Special Needs Trust for someone who receives government benefits. In fact, if such transfers of assets are not done with precision and knowledge, the trust could fall victim to the sixty month "Look-Back" rule."

Asset transfers such as these originated with middle-aged children who wanted to shield the assets of their elderly parents. It can be done, but if courts find the asset transfers were not properly done, they will consider these transfers to be "constructive fraud." In other words, if you divest yourself of assets in order to qualify for public assistance, a court could undo the irrevocable trust.

One alternative suggested by Laguna Hills attorney David McDowell is to use funds from a viaticum or ADB to buy a single pay annuity that pays a monthly allowance.

How can I find an attorney who is experienced and knowledgeable about estate planning and living trusts?

Not in the yellow pages. And not without sweat. Although the best choice is an attorney who specializes in Elder Law, Elder Law attorneys are a rare breed. You may need Sherlock Holmes to help you find one.

> Armond Budish, an expert on trusts, advises not to seek an attorney through the phone book or general advertising.
>
> "Your local bar association may have a referral service," adds Budish, "but use it only as a last resort."
>
> The reason: lawyers usually pay a fee to be on the referral list, and are not screened.

Take care to avoid inexperienced attorneys who offer to design a trust simply because they are hungry. A New Jersey couple made this mistake, when they sought an attorney to update their will in order to provide for a disabled adult daughter. They were quoted a fee of $800 to $900. But when the special needs trust was done, the cost came to $4,510.[11]

This attorney explained his far greater fee on the basis of time spent reviewing New Jersey law related to special benefits for the disabled. The lesson: Attorneys who don't regularly deal with families of handicapped children may charge for hours and hours of basic research. Or they may produce a flawed will or trust.

On the other hand, every attorney has to have a first client. According to Dave McDowell, who specializes in estate planning and trusts,[12]

> "Not many lawyers have ever done a Special Needs Trust. We would not have done the first one, if we didn't feel we could do it right. We told the client that it was our first time. We did extensive research, but didn't charge the client for our legal education. We also had help from the Bar Association. After drafting the documents, we went back and checked again, then had legal friends evaluate our work."

The following steps, compiled from several sources, should enable you to find a competent estate planning attorney:

- Ask an attorney who teaches probate or estate planning at a local law school. This attorney "may practice the specialty, or may be able to recommend someone who does."[13]

- Ask other professionals whom you trust (e.g., your accountant, doctor, clergyman).[14]

- When you ask for referrals, specify that you want a person experienced in dealing with the handicapped.

- Interview three attorneys who profess expertise in this specialized field. Many attorneys offer a free initial consultation.

Don't expect specific advice at the initial consultation. According to attorney McDowell, the purpose of these meetings is to assess if you have a problem, and if it's one the attorney is competent to handle.

If the problem requires research, ask how the attorney will go about this research, and if you'll be billed for research time.

- Ask when the attorney last set up an estate for an handicapped child — and how many in the past year. Since the law is ever changing, recent experience is more important than twenty years' experience. Seek "an attorney whose practice demands constant awareness of the relevant regulatory developments."[15]

• Ask how the funds will effect your (or your partner's) future eligibility for federal or state aid, especially means-based benefits like Supplemental Social Insurance (SSI) and Medicaid.

> Competence is not necessarily partner to experience. An experienced attorney who is not up on the law, or one who uses a boilerplate computer program, may draft a faulty trust. Since trust laws change radically and frequently, trusts should be reviewed every two years or they may become as valuable as last week's newspaper.

• When you find an attorney with whom you feel comfortable, ask for a fee agreement. A flat fee arrangement is preferable to an hourly fee. If the New Jersey couple had a written agreement for a flat fee, the attorney could not have raised the cost from several hundred to several thousand.

• Have the fee agreement mailed to you. This will give you time to review it without pressure. If there is anything in the agreement that is unclear, ask the attorney to revise (in plain English). If it states something you dislike, question the attorney about this. If s/he is not willing to strike the objectional issue, go on to someone else.

The insurer's check arrived the day my partner died. Since I'm executor and sole beneficiary, must I pay taxes on the ADB?

You have the right to cash the check, but this will make your task as executor very complicated. For one, it's likely you'll be required to file a final tax return. You may also be required to pay tax on those funds. Instead of getting into a mess, return the check to the insurer with a letter explaining why you want these funds restored to the policy. Enclose a copy of the death certificate. When the insurance is paid to you as beneficiary, it will be totally tax free.

> Most insurance companies have legal departments staffed with astute attorneys. They can provide factual information to you — at no charge.

Like all other incidents in this book, this is based on a true story. I learned of it while preparing the final tax return for Rick's deceased partner. Rick was relieved to learn he would get a refund from withholding taxes his partner had paid. He said, "I hope it's large enough to pay the attorney who billed me $350."

"For what?"

"I didn't know what to do with the insurer's check. The lawyer wrote a cover letter and sent it back to the insurance company, and billed me $350."

Had Rick known, he could have done this himself — for the cost of a postage stamp.

My partner's viaticum arrived two days after he died. I'm executor and sole beneficiary. What should I do?

Until the insurance department tackles this issue, you'll have to keep the viaticum. The 15 day grace period for canceling the sale doesn't apply to you. Check the closing papers. There's a provision requiring the agreement be kept in force, in the event the viator dies during the transfer period.

Under current law, the viatical settlement is taxable to the viator. You'll have to file a final tax return for your partner, and declare the settlement. But don't overlook any deductions available to reduce the tax. Since it was a final illness, it's likely your partner had huge medical expenses.

Can I be forced to sell my insurance in order to qualify for government (public) benefits?

No. The government's position in regard to living benefits from life insurance is this: The *potential* to receive these benefits is not considered an available resource.[16]

In addition, states that enacted viatical regulation include in their statutes a prohibition against compelling terminally ill insureds to sell their life insurance.

I want my insurance to go to my child. If I declare bankruptcy, can I be forced to sell the policy?

Thomas McCormack, an acknowledged expert on government benefits, and David Peterson, founder of Affording Care, addressed this very question in 1991:

> "It is easy to foresee cases in which creditors seek to compel terminally ill debtors or bankrupts to viaticate based on the argument that their life insurance policies are assets available for debt payment. The issues faced in such litigation will be, at the least, provocative and eclectic."[17]

Most states that regulate viatical contracts have statutory provisions to protect the terminally ill from being compelled to sell their life insurance. This is yet another reason to support viatical regulation.

* * *

END NOTES

1. Prop. Reg. §1.7702-2(e). See, 1996 Tax Facts on Life Insurance, NU Law Services, The National Underwriter, Cincinnati, OH.

2. Thomas P. McCormack, author of The AIDS Benefits Handbook (Yale University Press, 1990), served as benefits policy specialist with the U.S. Department of Health and Human Services, and with the National Association of People With AIDS (NAPWA). A resident of Washington, D.C., McCormack is on the advisory board of Affording Care, Inc., the New York based nonprofit organization, founded by David Peterson.

3. IRS Pub. 596, p.6.

4. See IRS instructions for Form 1040, Line 6c (dependents).

5. Ibid.

6. Total taxable income includes viatical settlement plus social security benefits plus any other taxable income. Nontaxable income includes life insurance benefits received as a beneficiary, interest on municipal bonds, gifts, etc.

7. Box 5 on the SSA.

8. "Estate Planning for the Disabled: A Complex Problem," Richard W. Fee, Insurance Sales, June 1990. Fee recently co-authored a text and workbook, Planning for the Future — with L. Mark Russell, Arnold E. Grant, Suzanne M. Joseph. American Publishing Co. Available from Nolo bookstore ($24.95 each).

9. Nolo Press (Berkeley, CA) publishes self-help law books and software and distributes quality self-help law books from other publishers. Their 24-hour phone number: (800) 992-6665.

10. Most lawyers are not familiar with trusts. Among those that have some knowledge, few are familiar with state and federal laws regarding the disabled.

11. "Care Required In Parents' Plans for the Disabled," Christopher J. Chipello, Wall Street Journal, August 8, 1988.

12. McDowells's law partner is Marcia Ellsworth.

13. Ibid.

14. "The Multi-Purpose Trust," Armond D. Budish, Modern Maturity, August-September 1991.

15. Chipello, Ibid.

16. Letter dated October 2, 1990, authored by Associate Regional Administrator for Medicaid Laurence L. McDonough of the Sacramento, California Region IX office. A copy of the letter was provided to the author by Per Larson.

17. "'Living Benefits' for the Insured, Terminally Ill Client: A Remarkable New Resource with Tax, SSI, and Medicaid Implications." McCormack, Thomas and Peterson, David. Clearinghouse Review, April 1991, p. 1348-1357.

Chapter 9

Look Before You Leap

Some people think of viatical settlements as lottery winnings. The opposite is true: Viatication should be a last resort choice. Don't sell your insurance until you've considered various alternatives. Then use the checklist to decide if this is the right time to sell.

Why should viatication be a last resort choice?

Primarily because it's a losing proposition. Viatical providers take steep discounts. As a result, few people get more than 70 percent of face value, many get closer to 50 percent, and a few have been offered 30 percent. Here's one example:

Nancy T. had a three year life expectancy and was desperately in need of funds. She applied to Lifetime Options, a funding firm that accommodates life expectancies up to five years through their "Extended Purchase Plan." Carl Holland explained this plan:

"The purchase price is greatly reduced. Perhaps as much as 20 or 30 percent for a five year life expectancy. But this makes it possible for people with immediate needs to get money — people who can't wait. They can get 20 or 30 percent now."

When Nancy sold her $100,000 policy, she was paid $25,000. But the following year, when her health was worse, she was out of money.

"She can come back to us," said Holland, "and ask us to review her medical condition. If we find it's changed — if we find there's a distinct decrease — we'll give her more money. We'll say, 'Looking at you today as if it were the first time, we would have given you 75 percent. So we'll give you an additional 50 percent.'"

Might Nancy do better to sell the balance of her policy at ye ole auction?

"In that case," said Holland, "the viator can buy back the policy for the amount we paid, plus interest. She'll know in advance what the loan borrowing rate is. She knows what it'll cost to buy back the policy and perhaps find another company that will give her more money. But we get first right of refusal."

In other words, if Lifetime Options refuses to refinance, you can buy back the policy and then shop it in the marketplace.

Here's another example of selling too soon:

> "A young woman with terminal cancer needs $30,000, so she viaticates her life insurance policy. She receives $65,000 on the $100,000 policy. Had the insurance remained in force, her

> parents would have received $100,000. If they had lent their daughter the $30,000, they would still have $70,000."[1]

Once you've sold your policy, that's it. At the same time, it's highly likely you won't die on schedule — especially if you have funds to relieve your financial woes and buy proper medical care. But once the policy is gone, what will you do?

Sometimes an alternative presents itself — when heirs are asked to sign the waiver of their rights to insurance proceeds.

"It is often at this point that beneficiaries will start proposing loans as an alternative, without the insured having to ask."[2]

Loans! Not only tax-free, they don't eat up the entire policy.

Where can I get a commercial loan?

Not from traditional sources — directly, that is. When I researched bank loans for a viatical client and described the loan as collateralized by life insurance death benefits, bank officials gulped, gulped again, then reacted as if I were blabbering some mumbo jumbo. With one exception — a bank officer who referred me to one of the bank's attorneys. This attorney, a woman, knew exactly what I was talking about. Her bank had considered getting into the viatical business but decided against it. The reasons: legally too complicated, too much paperwork, and too expensive. And no, she didn't offer a commercial loan.

However, a friend or relative may qualify for a commercial loan, then re-lend these funds to you.

Another possibility: Viatical funding firms that offer commercial loans. This is available through National Medical

Funding (the Pardo/Life Partners affiliate), and through The Viaticum Fund.

The Viaticum Fund calls their loan, LifeWise. They claim to have spent in excess of $250,000 to design a credit line that would meet approval in most states. According to Judy Larsen, Vice President of LifeWise, viators may choose between a lump sum or an equity line from which they may draw increments of at least $5,000. Interest is set at credit card rates (currently 18.5 percent), and applies only to the amount withdrawn.

LifeWise is a non-recourse loan, meaning that total debt cannot exceed the face value of the policy. The advantage is that other assets are protected, if you outlive your life expectancy (in which case interest could climb astronomically).

> What if the funding company becomes insolvent? What if they run out of money and skip town after you receive two loan payments? Your policy will be gone with the wind, and you'll have little to show for it.

What about a situation in which an insured receives only two or three payments, then dies? LifeWise deducts loan principal and interest, and forwards the remaining death benefit to the insured's beneficiaries.

In the event that an insured changes his mind (perhaps wins a lottery, or finds the disease in remission), both principal and interest can be repaid without penalty, and the policy returned to the insured.

Question: What's the likelihood that you'll be able to finance a buy-back?

Question: Is the LifeWise program legal? Installment payments are prohibited by New York viatical law. In California, according to an attorney with the DOI, the loan program wouldn't be regulated by the Department of Insurance unless it violates insurance law: if the funder named itself beneficiary and provided annuity-type income.

> What's the likelihood that a viatical firm will be around — and solvent enough — to continue making payments? Remember the short life expectancy of most viatical firms (Chapter 2)? And incidents of installments that never were paid in full (Chapter 5)?

Another type of viatical loan is offered by Accelerated Benefits Capital (in Michigan) — but only to Canadian viators, through its Montreal office. A banking institution acts as conduit for funds, which provides additional security for viators. When the loan is closed, funds are deposited with the bank, and the bank is directed to execute the agreement with the viator, if ABC should go out of business for any reason.

The more I learned about viatical loans the more curious I became about LifeWise. Then a client, Greg, applied to viatical firms, including LifeWise. After sending back the application, he never heard another word from them. Since Greg had listed me on the application as one of his friends, long after he had his viaticum (from another funder), Judy Larsen phoned me, to explain her firm's silence: They were unable to get the physician to return the questionnaire, and she was reluctant to phone the client to ask his assistance.

When another client, Pat, came for tax preparation, he showed me a LifeWise advertisement clipped from a gay publication. Pat was intrigued for two reasons: no tax problems to worry him, and he wouldn't have to sell his entire policy. What would you have advised?

You guessed it: Check the alternatives.

What alternatives?

Split your policy into bite sized pieces, then sell one of the smaller policies. Remember the young woman with terminal cancer? To get $30,000, she viaticated a policy worth $100,000, and was paid 65 percent ($65,000). Had she split her policy, to have two policies, each with a face value of $50,000, she could have viaticated one and saved the other. The first policy would have paid the same percentage — 65 — and given her $32,500. Upon her death, the second policy would have paid $50,000 to her parents. Total payout for both policies would have been $82,500 (instead of $65,000).

Or, she might have viaticated the second policy in a later year. Since her life expectancy would be shorter, there would have been a smaller discount. Assuming she was paid 80 for the second policy, she would have received $40,000. Added to the first viaticum of $32,500, total payout is $72,500.

To split your policy, contact your insurance agent for guidance. If you don't have an agent, phone the home office directly. You want to be sure that the smaller policies carry the original issue date, so that you don't have to satisfy a new incontestability period.[3] This shouldn't be a problem for the insurer, since they don't incur more risk.[4]

Before you try this, check with your beneficiaries. They may be able to finance a loan, using your policy as collateral.

What if beneficiaries don't have funds for a loan?

You may have an employer who is able (and willing) to make such a loan. In exchange, you could name the employer as beneficiary for the amount of the loan — plus interest.

Approaching an employer may have unforeseen results. A client who works at an Orange county hospital advised a terminally ill co-worker to ask the Human Resources Department about a loan. When he inquired, he learned that the hospital had just added Accelerated Death Benefits to their self-funded insurance plan.

If you turn to family members and they don't have funds, instead, they may qualify for a bank loan which they could pass on to you.

How can parents get a loan?

Parents and grandparents can use the equity in their homes via a second mortgage, a home equity credit line, or reverse mortgage. Second mortgages are like first mortgages: they pay a lump sum, and principal and interest are repaid monthly. An equity credit line may give you the same amount as a second mortgage, but funds are withdrawn as needed, and you may get away with interest-only payments until the note is due. Both types of loans are subject to the same ceilings for tax deductible mortgage interests.

If your family chooses any loan program, advise them to avoid those that include pre-payment penalties.

What is a reverse mortgage?

Reverse mortgages allow senior citizens to tap the equity in their homes without having to sell and move out. Los Angeles Times financial writer, Carla Lazzareschi, described the process:

> "A lending institution makes the homeowner a loan based on the borrower's age — the minimum ranges from 62 to 65 — and the property's appraised value. After taking its loan fees and points up front, the institution pays the loan, either in monthly installments, in a lump sum, or as a line of credit, for as long as the borrower continues living in the home. The loan balance, which is actually the amount dispersed plus interest and loan fees, is repaid when the house is sold by the owner or his heirs."[5]

This is a costly short-term loan. Loan fees and points are taken at the outset — on the full potential loan amount. For some programs annualized loan costs may exceed 20 percent in the early years.[6]

Then there is the issue of how much money the homeowner can pocket. The amount varies widely:

- FHA loans are limited to $151,250
- Chicago-based Household Bank offers an equity line limited to $250,000
- San Francisco-based Transamerica Corporation limits loans to $600,000 in equity
- Fannie Mae has a new "Home Keeper" plan that allows up to $104,800 "provided the borrower agrees to share with the

lender 10 percent of the home's value when the home is sold (as well as repaying the loan)."[7]

- The U.S. Department of Housing and Urban Development (HUD) sponsors a Home Equity Conversion Mortgage for people over age 60.

Another area to watch for, according to attorney Herbert I. Rosenkrantz, of Calabasas, California, is the "trap for the unwary contained in many but not all reverse mortgages notes and/or trust deeds."[8]

This "trap" allows lenders to consider a "move out" lasting more than a certain time as lack of intent to return. The move out clause allows lenders to "give themselves the right to foreclose in the event of a move to a nursing home."[9] The time period for the move-out may be as short as twelve months. (Note: Fannie Mae includes the move-out/right to foreclose provision in their contracts.)

As with viatical settlements, be fully informed and check several sources before you make a decision. One reference source, "Your New Retirement Nest Egg," by Ken Scholen,[10] is highly touted by attorney Robert J. Bruss, who authors a real estate column for the Los Angeles Times.

Now for the grab bag of questions:

Question 1: Is this employment discrimination?

Brian asked his employer about converting his group term to an individual policy. Now the employer knew that Brian had a life-threatening illness. Instead of permission to convert his policy, he was given a different job — one that kept him isolated.

If an employer, supervisor, or co-workers learn that you have a life-threatening illness and conclude that you are no longer fit to do the work you did that morning, that's clear-cut discrimination. The following are other instances of health discrimination:

• An employer is erroneously concerned that you harbor an infectious or contagious disease and isolates your work space

• An employer changes your job because s/he erroneously fears that your illness might cause you:

(a) to be injured if you continue doing the current work

(b) to have frequent absences when the position calls for availability on the premises

• The employer changes the job description, so that you no longer can perform the "essential" functions, and therefore no longer are suited to the work.

Health discrimination is not limited to people who suffer life threatening illnesses. Relatives, friends, associates, medical providers, and volunteers who work with these individuals may be subject to employment discrimination. For this reason, all these groups are covered by the Americans with Disability Act.

Question 2: What can I do about employment discrimination?

Employment discrimination against the disabled is prohibited by Title I of the ADA. The law applies to private employers who have at least fifteen employees each day for at least twenty weeks of the year.

Peter M., a tax client who had AIDS, had a clear-cut case of employment discrimination. To spare him the stress of telling his story over and over, I went lawyer shopping for him. Three private sector attorneys who specialize in discrimination, and an attorney at the Public Law Center in Santa Ana advised the very same thing . . .

Sometimes the mere threat of a lawsuit causes an employer to shape up, or to provide accommodations for the disability. But it's more likely a potential lawsuit will worsen work conditions, sometimes to the point where the individual cannot continue. This further jeopardizes the client: when work stops, income stops. Then there's the problem of continuing medical benefits. COBRA-continuation of medical benefits is far more costly, and generally ends after eighteen months.

Each lawyer pointed to the stress of going through a lawsuit. A lawsuit could be more stressful than what the client endured at work.

If you don't have a choice — because your employment is terminated — don't take any action without expert advice. For example, if you apply for disability benefits, it's possible the courts will bar you from an ADA Discrimination suit.

A federal judge in Philadelphia dismissed a lawsuit brought by an assistant manager of a Disney store in Cherry Hill, N.J., who suffered from AIDS. The reason: He had applied for social security disability benefits after being fired.[11]

Question 3: If I disclose my illness, will I risk being terminated?

Perhaps the most difficult situation occurs when an employer terminates or changes the job description due to mixed motives. One motive may be discrimination, but the employer may claim a second, legitimate motive (e.g., cost savings by combining two jobs in one). If you think you have cause for legal action, this is how to prepare yourself:

- Read company benefits books — especially those sections about continuing medical and life insurance after employment termination
- Ask a trusted friend to visit personnel (or human resources) for you, to get applicable forms
- Make all disclosures in writing
- Have proof of disclosure; use certified mail, return receipt
- Be certain you have a trusted witness — or two; or tape record conversations with supervisors and employers
- Keep a notebook of all relevant matters (e.g., telephone calls, meetings, etc.)
- Follow-up with letters, or request confirmation in writing. "Do not rely on verbal assurances alone!"[12]
- Save copies of everything
- Have a back-up plan: seek other employment; apply for unemployment compensation; file EEOC discrimination complaint; file ADA civil lawsuit
- Note: Take care to observe cut-off dates for continuation of benefits and any long-term disability that may be available.

* * *

Before Viaticating: A Checklist

- ☐ Other assets to sell first (non-highly appreciated)
- ☐ All possibilities for a loan have been explored
- ☐ Accelerated Death Benefits have been verified
- ☐ Disability waiver of premium is (or is not) available
- ☐ Evaluated all risks of converting from group term
- ☐ Evaluated risk to government benefits
- ☐ Evaluated tax effect, and whether it would be better to viaticate next year
- ☐ Evaluated choice of policies to sell: the one with higher premiums, or without a disability waiver
- ☐ Consulted insurer about splitting large policy into two (or more) smaller policies

* * *

END NOTES

1. "Reservations for the Final Journey," Peg Downey. Winning Strategies, Summer 1994.

2. Ibid.

3. Original date is important. You want the policy to be past the two-year incontestability period.

4. The insurer is at risk for the amount of death benefit.

5. "Money Talk: A Few Caveats on Reverse Mortgages," Carla Lazzareschi. Los Angeles Times, December 3, 1995.

6. "Shop Around if Considering a Reverse Loan," Kenneth R. Harney. Los Angeles Times, March 10, 1996.

7. Ibid.

8. "Thinking of a Reverse Mortgage? There's Something You Should Know." Letter from atty Rosenkrantz published in Los Angeles Times, Nov. 19, 1995.

9. Ibid.

10. Available through the National Center for Home Equity Conversion, 7373 147th St. West, Ste. 115, Apply Valley, MN 55124. Phone (800) 247-6553. The book sells for $24.95.

11.Frances A. McMorris, Courts May Bar ADA Discrimination Suits, Wall Street Journal, September 8, 1995, B14.

12. This list was adapted from the outline of a presentation to the AIDS Equity League by attorney Mitchell Katine of Williams, Birnberg & Anderson, Houston, Texas. The outline was provided to the author by Rick Perry, President of Life Today.

AFTERWORD

This book makes a powerful case that reform, in the nature of consumer protections and disclosures, is vital in the Viatical Settlement arena. Consider just some of the public policy issues raised in this volume:

Public policy issue #1: Who determines which insureds are entitled to Accelerated Death Benefits?

Insurers decide which policies include the rider. Shouldn't ADB be required on all new life insurance policies?

This can be accomplished either by mandate from the individual states, or through people power: the might of the dollar. If the public refused to buy policies that lacked this feature, insurers would be forced to add it to all newly issued policies. In order for this to occur, clear disclosure of Accelerated Death Benefits (or the lack of it) should be required in all life insurance sales.

Public policy issue #2: Should viatical licensees be required to have knowledge of insurance law and contracts?

Most viatical providers give advice to viators about conversion rights and other insurance matters. Since they act as if they have such knowledge, insurance departments should require licensees to demonstrate that they do, in fact, have a basic knowledge of insurance.

Public policy issue #3: Is it in the public interest to require disclosure of referral fees?

New York forbids viatical settlement companies from paying, or offering to pay, a finder's fee or commission to any person who provides medical, legal, or financial planning services to the viator. New York also requires disclosure of all fees related to the purchase of a viator's life insurance. Shouldn't all viators have similar protection in all states?

Public policy issue #4: Is it in the public interest to allow brokers to withhold purchase offers from funding firms that pay low commissions? Shouldn't all offers be brought to the table so that viators may choose the one most favorable to them?

Public policy issue #5: Should it be illegal for viatical providers to cancel an offer after it has been accepted?

It is illegal — according to the law of contracts. The question should be: does this law need to be reiterated and enforced in viatical regulations?

Public policy issue #6: Should insurance carriers be permitted to own viatical companies?

If a state determines that a conflict of interest exists for insurance agents who market viatical contracts, how is it possible for insurers to avoid this conflict? I think insurers should have to offer Accelerated Death Benefits and *not* be allowed to own a viatical company.

Public policy issue #7: Does viatical regulation provide an effective means of protecting the public?

Viatical regulation offers benefits far beyond the control of business practices of the viatical providers. Regulation allows states to exempt pre-death benefits from state income taxes; to exempt these funds from money-judgments (including bankruptcy); and to forbid public-assistance agencies, health care facilities or providers, from requiring viatication as a condition of eligibility.

In regard to direct protection of the public, regulation prevents viatical companies from assuming tasteless names (e.g., The Grim Reaper). Beyond these areas, it is questionable whether viatical regulation is effective in deterring unethical or illegal practices.

Some states have viatical regulation but no control (Texas, for example). Some states have viatical regulation but erratic enforcement (California, for example). And there are states with no viatical regulation whatsoever — the *majority* of the nation has no regulation!

Why would some states choose not to enact viatical regulation? The main reason is: relatively small population. If viatical providers decide that the population is too small to warrant the expense of licensure, viators may lose the opportunity to sell their policies to legitimate firms.

This is not an either-or choice. A third option for these states is to adopt viatical providers who are qualified to do business in the two states with the most stringent requirements: California and New York. Reciprocity would offer additional advantages:

1. Licenses would be portable, and licensing requirements standardized. This would make compliance easier and less expensive for viatical providers, most of whom do transact business beyond the borders of their home state.

2. Licensing would become more effective as a deterrent to illegal practices. If a provider who is guilty of serious violations forfeits its license in one state, reciprocal states would similarly revoke that provider's license.

Public policy issue #8: How can regulation effectively prevent illegal companies from operating within the state?

Illegal operators flourish because the rewards are great and the penalties small. In California, violations of viatical regulations are considered misdemeanors. The maximum penalty is ten thousand dollars: a peanut-sized penalty in an industry that begins counting revenues in six and seven figures.

States that are beleaguered with unauthorized companies could complain to the home states of these companies. Why doesn't this happen? One reason may be that not one viator has registered a formal complaint. Why not?

What terminally ill person has the stamina to get embroiled in complaint proceedings? Particularly if resolution won't occur until some future date beyond the individual's life expectancy.

We need to seek other solutions. If unauthorized firms flourish primarily because their targets are not aware that they are illegal, if most advisors to the terminally ill are similarly unaware of viatical regulation, then regulation and public education is the key to reform.

Secondly, the insurance industry should take steps to educate policyholders about Accelerated Death Benefits. Additionally, insurers should red-flag Absolute Assignment forms that assign policies to a firm or group of individuals. Before acting on this transfer request, insurers should notify the policyholder that there is an alternative (ADB), including the amount available, and the procedure and time required to access these benefits.

Third, the viatical industry should do these things:

1. When a new broker asks to contract with a funding firm, that firm should check with the DOI to learn if the broker has applied for a license.

2. Refuse to accept from unauthorized brokers, or place business with unauthorized funding firms.

America needs to control this new industry. In far too many states there is no control — leaving terminally ill people at the mercy of some pretty questionable business practices. The state insurance regulators — and particularly the National Association of Insurance Commissioners — had better see to it that this regulatory lapse is repaired.

Robert Hunter

Former Texas Insurance Commissioner

Director of Insurance, Consumer Federation of America

California Licensed Viatical Providers

Key:

Company; Principal; Location;

F = Funder B= Broker **Yr** = Year established

1: Face amount

(mini; maxi)

2: Life expectancy

3: Diseases accepted:

A = A (IDS)

C = C (ancer)

He = H (emophilia)

Ht = H (eart)

L = ALS

All= All the above

O = O (thers)

4: Policies accepted:

F = F (EGLI)

G = G (roup term)

P = P (artial sale)

Ir = Ir (revocable Beneficiary)

5a. For Funders:

Do you also broker on occasion? Y/N

5b. For Brokers: Do you sell to:

V(iatical) funding firms

PP(ension Plans)

I (ndividuals)

B (usiness investment trusts)

6: * = Licensed

**** = License pending**

State:

7: Source of clients:

M = M (agazine ads)

N = N (ewspaper ads)

V = V (iatical) firms

I = I (nsur. agents)

F = F (inancial planners)

A = A (ttys, accountants)

D = D (octors, other health providers)

S = S (ervice providers) Ex.: social workers

P = P (revious viators)

8. Trade Assoc.

VAA

NVA

American Life Resources

Kenneth M. Klein **F-1989**

New York, NY

(800) 750-3383

1: $10,000 - $1 million

2: to 3 yrs.

3: All diseases

4: All policies

5a: No

6: *CA, NY, TX

**WA, OR, KA, MN, NC

7: M N V I F A S P

8: VAA

Benefit Advocates

Nancy Cane **B-1992**

San Luis Obispo, CA

(800) 435-8891

1: $5,000- no max.

2: to 5 years

3. All diseases

4: All policies

5b: V

6: *CA, WA

**NY + all where required

7: M N V I F A D S

8: -

Dedicated Resources

Michael D. Zadoff **F-1989**

Del Ray Beach, FL

(800) 677-5026

1: $10,000 to $1 million

2: to 5 yrs.

3: All diseases + Structured Settlements

4: No partial

5a: No

6: *NY, CA

7: M N V I F A D S

8: -

Dignity Partners

Alan B. Perper **F-1992**

San Francisco, CA

(800) 716-3605

1: Any size

2: Any life exp.

3: All diseases

4: All policies

5a: No

6: *CA, WA

**All states where required

7: V and other referrals

8: VAA (a founder)

Fiedler Financial

Carole Fiedler **B-1994**

Sausalito, CA

(800) 905-0114

1: $10,000- no max

2: to 5 yrs.

3: All diseases

4: All policies

5b: V

6: *CA, WA

**TX

7: M N V A D S P

8: VAA

Individual Benefits

Ramon A. Vicente **B-1992**

Greensboro, NC

(800) 800-3264

1: $10,000- no max.

2: Any

3: All diseases

4: All policies

5b: V, PI, PP, BIT

6 *CA, WA, TX, NC

-

7: M N V I F

8: VAA

LifeAID

Alan E. Kannan **F-1992**

Encino, CA

(800) LIFEAID

1: $10,000- no max

2: to 3 yrs.

3: A

4: E, P

5a: Yes

6: *CA

-

7: M V U F A D P

8: -

Life Benefactors

Cale W. Carson **F-1993**

San Diego, CA

(800) 285-5152

1: $10,000 - $1 million

2: Any life exp.

3: All diseases

4: All policies

5a: Yes

6: *CA, WA

** NY, TX

7: M V F A S P

8: VAA

Life Entitlements

Geo. H. McLaughlin **F-1993**

New York, NY

(800) 420-1420

1: $15,000- no max.

2: 2 - 3 yrs.

3: A C Ht Leukemia

4: F P

5a: No

6: *CA, NY, WA

**TX

7: M N V I F A D S P

8: VAA

Lifetime Options

Craig Fishman **F-1991**

Arlington, VA

(800) 999-5419

1: $10,000 - $1 million

2: to 5 yrs.

3: A C

4: All policies

5a: No

6: *NY, CA

7: M N V F S P

8: VAA

Living Benefits

Kenneth M. Klein **F-1989**

New York, NY

(800) 750-3363

1: $10,000 - 1 million

2: to 36 yrs.

3: All diseases

4: All policies

5a: No

6: *CA, TX, NY

**WA, OR, KA, MN, NC

7: M N V I F A S P

8: VAA

Neuma

David-Irwin Binter **F-1991**

Skokie, IL; San Fr, CA

(800) 457-7828

1: $10,000 - $350,000

2: to 3 yrs.

3: All diseases

4: All policies

5a: Yes

6: *CA, NY, VT, WA

**OR, NC, TX, IN, LA

7: M N V I F A D S P

8: VAA

Page & Associates
Scott Page **F-1992**
Ft. Lauderdale, FL
(800) 572-4346
1: $10,000; no maxi
2: to 48 mos.
3: All diseases
4: All policies
5a: Y
6: *NY
**CA, WA
7: M N V I F A S
8: NVA (Pres.)

ViatiCare
Paul Moe **F-1993**
Minneapolish, MN
(800) 333-2249
1: No mini; no maxi
2: to 3 yrs.; some 48 mos.
3: All diseases
4: All policies
5a: No
6: *CA, MN
**All states where required
7: M N V I F A D S P
8: VAA

LifeWise (Viaticum Fund)
Mark Livingstone **F-1995**
Salt Lake City, UT
(800) 219-7385
1: No mini; no maxi
2: 0 - 60 mos.
3: A, C, L, COPD
4: F, E
5a: No
6: * CA
** TX
7: M N S
8: VAA

Three attempts were made to contact the principals, but the following companies did not respond to the survey:

Accelerated Benefits of WA
David Berman, M.D. **F-199x**
Sterling, VA 20165
(disconnected 800#)

Affirmative Lifestyles
Thomas W. Wallace **B-199x**
San Antonio, TX
(800) 876-2991

CA Licenses-Pending

Accelerated Benefits Capital

Robert L. Shear **F-1993**

Oak Park, MI and Montreal

(800) 327-8222

1: $10,000 to $350,000

2: to 4 yrs.

3: A C Ht

4: F E I, P (see notes)

5a: Yes

6: *WA

**CA TX

7: M N V F A S

8: VAA

Legacy Benefits

Meir Eliav **F-1991**

New York, NY

(800) 875-1000

1: $10,000 - $1 million

2: to 3 yrs.

3: All diseases

4: F E P

5a: Yes

6: *NY, WA

**CA, TX, NC, OR

7: M N V F S P

8: VAA

Life Today

Rick Perry **B/F-1991**

Houston, TX

(800) 554-2104

1: $10,000 - no max.

2: to 5 yrs.

3: A C H

4: All policies

5b: V funding firms only

6: -

**CA TX

7: M P AIDS organizations

8: -

National Medical Funding

Carmen J. Palmieri **F-1994**

San Diego, CA

(800) 700-7334

1: $10,000

2: $1,500,000

3: to 5 yrs.

4: All diseases

5a: Yes

6: -

**CA

7: M N V I F A D S P

8: NAPWA, BBB, Chamber

National Viator Reps.

David S. Landay **B-1992**

New York, NY

(800) 932-0050

1: Any

2: Any

3: All diseases

4: All policies

5b: V

6: *WA

**CA, NY, TX

7: All sources

8: VAA

Slome (**Access Program**)

Ansel A. Slome **B-1991**

Los Angeles, CA

(800) 235-6411

1: $10,000 - no max.

2: to 4 yrs.

3: All diseases

4: All policies

5b: V

6: *CA

**WA

7: M A S

8: -

Renfrew Financial

Roderick Renfrew **B-1995**

West Hollywood, CA

(888) 271-1295 (toll free)

1: $10,000 - no max.

2: to 5 yrs.

3: All diseases

4: F E P

5b: V only

6: -

**CA

7: M N F A D S P

8: -

Viatical Clearing House

Deborah Rhoades **B-1992**

Loveland, OH

(800) 969-0509

1: $10,000 - no max.

2: to 4 yrs.

3: All policies

4: All diseases

5b: V, PP

6: -

**CA

7: M N V I F D S P

8 NVA

Viaticus

(800) 390-1390 **B-1994**

1: Any min./max.

2: To 7 yrs.

3: All diseases

4: All policies

5: *NY, VT, WA

**CA, IN, KA, OR, NC, ND, TX (all states where required)

6: M V I F A D S

also, Benefits Managers

7: VAA

8: No

Wilbanks & Assoc.

Scott Wilbanks **B-1995**

San Francisco, CA

(800) 644-6032

1: No mini; no maxi

2: to 4 yrs.

3: All diseases

4: All policies

5b: V

6: -

**CA, NY

7: F A D S P

8: -

The following companies were granted licenses but no longer are in business:

1. Medicap Viatical Stt. Co.
2. Assured Lifetime Benefits of Illinois
3. Eterna Benefits
4. Viatical Settlements Funding

The following companies operated under license-pending status but no longer are in business:

1. Ability Life Trust
2. Markom Resources, Inc.

Note: Robert Shear (Acclerated Benefits Cap.), explained his reply to Question #4: "We accept partial sales in states other than California. In California a portion of the death benefits can be paid to an insured's beneficiary only if the irrevocable beneficiary is listed on the insurance."

Universal Application/Questionnaire for Viatical Settlement

PERSONAL INFORMATION

Date:____

Name:____

Home Address:____________________________________

Current State Of Residency:__________________________

Home Phone:________________________Fax:________

Date ofBirth:____________________________________

Place of Birth:___________________________________

Social Security Number:____________________________

Driver's License Number:_________________State:________

Present Employer:_________________________________

Employer Address:________________________________

Employer Phone/Fax:______________________________

List any disease-specific support Groups, public benefits or other assistance or organizations assisting me:

____

____

____

Personal/Professional Acquaintances:

____

____

____

____

____

MEDICAL HISTORY

Current Medical Condition:________________________________

____

____

____

____

____

____

Current Medications/Therapies:____________________________

____

____

____

____

Date I Became Aware of Illness:____________________________

____

Attending Physician:____

Address:____

Phone:______________________________ **Fax:**____________________

Other Physicians Seen Within Past 24 Months:

(Name/Address/Phone):______________________________________

____

Hospitals:____

____

____

____

____

LIFE INSURANCE POLICY INFORMATION

Life Insurance Company:______________________________

Date Policy Issued:______________________________

Type Of Policy:______________________________

Plan Of Insurance:______________________________

Amount Of Coverage:______________________________

Policy Number:______________________________

Is There Cash Value?______________________________

Amount:______________________________

Are There Outstanding Loans?_Amount:______________________

Are Premiums Currently Paid By Disability Waiver Rider?______

Amount Of Premium:________________**Mode:**________________

Has Policy Ever Been Lapsed Or Reinstated:________________

List Present And Previous Beneficiaries:______________________

____

____

____

____

Insur. Company's Customer Service Phone Number:____________

____

Is This A Group Policy?______________

Have You Researched Any Potential Living Benefits____________

Or Accelerated Benefits Offered By The Insur. Company?_______

____

Have You Applied for A Viatical Settlement of This Policy With Another Company?:______________________________

AUTHORIZATION TO RELEASE MEDICAL RECORDS

I authorize any physician, medical practitioner, hospital or medically-related facility, insurance company, or other institution or person(s) having any of my medical records, to release, by facsimile and/or mail, all such medical records to **(VIATICAL PROVIDER NAME)**, and/or their authorized representative(s).

Medical records shall include all past, present, or future medical information or knowledge of medical information, medical reports, physical examination reports, hospital reports, laboratory reports, or x-ray reports relating to me or my health, including any HIV or psychological information.

This Authorization shall be valid for thirty six months from the date hereof. A photocopy and/or facsimile of this Authorization shall be as valid as the original.

X____

Insured's Signature Date

____

Type or Print Name Social Security #

____________________ ____________________

Witness Signature Witness Signature

____________________ ____________________

Type or Print Name Type or Print Name

Authorization To Release Policy Information

I, ___(your full name)______ , the owner/insured, hereby authorize _(your insurer)_____________ the issuer of insurance policy number _(policy #)_insuring the life of _(your name)__ to release to _(funding firm or broker name)__________ or its authorized representative(s), any and all information concerning this policy. A photocopy or facsimile of this document shall be as valid as the original.

X____

Insured's Signature Date

____

Type or Print Name Social Security #

______________________ ______________________

Witness Signature Witness Signature

______________________ ______________________

Type or Print Name Type or Print Name

GLOSSARY

Absolute Assignment— The transfer of ownership rights to another party

Accelerated Death Benefits (ADB)— Pre-death benefits paid to a terminally ill insured by an insurance carrier

Assignable— Allows transfer to another party

Association insurance— Insurance for groups with a common interest (e.g., sports or profession)

Beneficiary— The person(s) named to receive the death benefits

Broker— A viatical provider who assists viators with finding a buyer and negotiating a price

Cash out— To cancel an insurance policy in exchange for its net cash surrender value

Convert— Transfer from group to individual ownership

Death benefit— The amount paid to a beneficiary. Also known as face value or face amount

Decreasing term— Term insurance in which the death benefit reduces over time (e.g., mortgage insurance)

Disability waiver— A rider that excuses premium payments when an insured has been disabled for longer than six months

Escrow— A trust account at a financial institution

Evidence of insurability— Information about health, occupation, lifestyle, habits, income, net worth and other insurance

FEGLI— Federal Employees Government Life Insurance

Funding sources— Direct buyers of life insurance death benefits. Also known as funding firms or capitalization firms

Grace period— The time allowed for an insured to change his/her mind

Graded life— Life insurance designed for people with serious health problems; pays lower benefits in early years if death is from sickness

Guaranteed Insurability Option (GIO)— The right to increase the death benefit without evidence of insurability

Guaranteed issue life— see graded life

Incontestability period— The two year period in which an insurance contract can be voided for cause by an insurer

Irrevocable— Cannot be changed

Lapse— Ceases to be in force, as an insurance policy when the premium was not paid beyond the grace period force

Legal competency— of sound mind

Maturity value disability clause— A condition of employee group term insurance that allows insureds who are totally and permanently disabled prior to age sixty to receive the full face value of their insurance

Offer in Compromise— An offer to IRS to pay a percentage of the tax due, and have the balance excused

Ordinary life— Permanent, whole life or cash value insurance

Policy loan— Funds borrowed from a life insurance company using the cash value of the policy as collateral

Policyholder— The owner of an insurance policy

Premium— The payment required to keep a policy in force

PLWA— Person Living With AIDS

PWA— Person with AIDS

Reinstated— After a policy entered its grace period, the premium was paid and the policy was put back in force

Rescind— Cancel

Rider— A provision in an insurance contract that changes the benefits

SGLI— Servicemen's/women's Government Life Insurance

S.S.D.I.— Social Security Disability Insurance

S.S.I.— Supplemental social insurance; a means-based benefit

Term insurance— Life insurance without cash value. Premiums increase upon renewal.

Underwriting— The process of evaluating financial risk

Universal Life— A cash value policy that combines term insurance with a savings or investment feature. Also known as Flexible Premium Adjustable Life Insurance

Variable Life— similar to Universal Life except that the policyholder controls where the savings portion is invested

Waive— To excuse, as premiums or tax penalties

Waiver of premium— Premium payments are excused by an insurer when the insured has been totally disabled for six months

Whole life— Cash value, permanent life insurance, usually with level premiums payable for life

VGLI— Veteran's Government Life Insurance

Viatical settlement— The payment made in exchange for the beneficiary rights to an insured's life insurance policy

Viaticum— A viatical settlement

Viator— The insured who contracts for the sale of a life insurance policy

Viaticate— To sell a life insurance policy

INDEX

A

Absolute Assignment, 4, 125
Accelerated Benefits of Washington, 78, 187
Accelerated Benefits Corp (FLA), 83
Accelerated Benefits Capital, 83, 84, 91, 167, 182
Accelerated Death Benefits, 7-16, 28, 30, 47, 76-80, 85, 116, 130-132, 134, 139, 153, 140, 143, 159
Access, 36, 127, 183
Accidental Death and Dismemberment, 128
ADA, 174
ADB, *see* Accelerated Death Benefits
Adult disabled child, 146
Advocate, 54n.5
Affording Care, *see* Peterson, David
AIDS pandemic, 74-76
American Life Resourc, 8, 31n.4, 99, 100, 184
Application, 22, 25, 42, 58, 136
Assoc insurance, 6, 7, 66, 125
Attorneys, 156-158
Auction, 19, 61, 166
Authorization, 22, 26, 27, 36, 42, 57, 59
Ayoob, Nancy, 97, 101, 105-106

B

Bankruptcy, 58, 160
Beneficiary, 5, 6, 11, 16, 20, 62, 126, 128, 136, 153, 167, 171
Benefit Advocates, 81, 184
Benefit Handbook, 58, 67, 126, 127
Brokers, 11, 15, 19, 21-24, 34, 35, 42, 45-54, 59, 63, 95
Buyers, 47

C

California 18, 27, 33, 35, 39-41, 52, 67, 78-88, 96, 101, 105-106, 112, 118, 142
DOI 3, 10, 21, 88, 102, 102, 107, 116
Cancel (rescind), 26, 67-69, 80
Cash flow, 79, 29, 67
Cash out, 17, 123
Cash value, 17, 48, 67, 124
Checklist, 175
Competency, legal, 63-65
Confidentiality, 20, 37, 80, 107
Connecticut Mutual, 77

Conversion, 5-7, 12, 26, 66, 135
  conditions, 127
  cut-off date, 132
Coping, 54n.4
Credit Life, 72

D

Death benefit, 3-5, 7, 10, 47, 48, 123, 124, 127, 128, 130, 131, 135, 136, 165
  face amount, 4
  face value, 4
Dedicated Resources, 184
Dementia, 74
Diagnosis, 8, 14, 55, 78, 135
Dignity Partners, 38, 50, 55n.3, 68, 80, 82, 100, 102, 142n.3, 184
Disability benefit, 175
Disability waiver, 18, 67, 128
Disclosure, 21, 23, 67, 78, 80, 175
Discount, 8, 25, 78, 81, 127
Discount rates, 10
Discretionary Trust, 154
Discrimination, 7, 171-174
Diseases, 8
Dividends, 17, 143
DOI, *see* California
Domestic partner, 147
Driver's license, 59
Dual licensing, 82, 115

E

Earned Income Credit, 146, 147
EEOC, 176
Employer, 6, 25, 171, 173
Employment, 58
  discrimination, 7, 171-174
Empty claims, 39, 40
End notes, 31, 43, 54, 70, 87, 118, 138, 161, 176
Endowment policies, 75
Escrow, 21, 40, 60, 81, 109
Estate planning, 153-160
Evidence
  of insurability, 6, 48, 129, 136
Executor, 159
Extended death benefits, 128
Extended term insurance, 124

F

Face amount, 9, 124, 165
  and brokers, 49
  decreasing, 7, 128, 131
  increasing, 4, 48, 128
Face value, *see* face amount, or death benefit
Fees, 20, 21, 23, 49, 50, 51, 67, 94, 158
FEGLI, 129-131, 135,

48, 67, 69, 84, 124
Unlicensed firms, 39, 78, 82-84
US News & World Rpt, 32n.5, 51, 54n.5, 75, 106

V

Variable Life, 48, 67, 124
Vermont, 96
VGLI, 129, 130
Viatical Assoc of Amer (VAA), 70n.1, 100
Viatical Clearing House, 46, 47, 54, 189
Viatical regulation, 18, 49, 99
ViatiCare, 34, 38, 39, 42, 62, 72n.3, 187
Viaticum Fund, The, 62, 166, 187
Viaticus, 38, 85, 190

W

Waiver of premium, 18, 67, 128, 136
Wall Street Journal, 32n.5, 80n.15, 108
Washington Blade, The, 103-105
Washington Business Journal, 89n.4
Washington Viatical Network, 83
Washington state, 83
Whole life, 6, 17, 48, 124
Wilbanks & Assoc, 35, 36, 51, 61, 190
Worth, 75n.1

Order Form

Universal Application and Authorization forms (size 8x11): **free.**
Simply send an SASE (stamped, self-addressed envelope) with postage: 2 first class stamps.

Computer disk (Universal Application and Authorization forms)
Send check or money order for $10.00, payable to Bialkin Books, at the address below.

Viatical/ADB Newsletter.

Was the book helpful? Do you have questions that were not answered? Your comments and questions will help others, through the newsletter.

The Viatical/ADB Newsletter will include changes in viatical and related insurance law, as well as an annual "Mr. Blackwell's Best- and Worst-Dressed" list of insurers and viatical providers. Send correspondence, audio tapes, insurer brochures — anything that supports kudos for the good guys, or kicks for the bad ones.

The first edition of the newsletter is free: send a self-addressed, stamped envelope. The first 50 people to request the newsletter, as well as anyone who sends a comment, question, or evidence about an insurer or viatical provider, will receive four free issues.

Audio tapes of this book are planned.

If you or someone you know is interested in the audio version, please send name and address to:

G. Wolk
Bialkin Books
23581-G Alicia Pkwy., #336C
Laguna Hills, CA 92653

☐ Universal Application & Authorization forms. Enclosed is a SASE with 2 first class stamps

☐ Computer disk with the above forms ($10.00 check or money order enclosed) IBM compat:____ Mac____

☐ Viatical/ADB Newsletter (SASE enclosed)

Please send this order to:

NAME:______________________________

ADDRESS:______________________________

CITY/STATE:____________________ZIP:__________

FEGLI (cont'd) tax on, 140
Fiedler Financial, 46, 49, 135, 185
Financial stability, 80, 127
Fly-by-night (illegal), 78, 82-84
Funding firms, 34, 38, 42, 49, 52, 63, 68, 70

G

Government insur,
FEGLI, 129, 135, 140
SGLI, 129
VGLI, 129
Grace period, 26, 69, 125
Graded life, 136, 137
Grim Reaper, The, 71
Group insur, 5-7, 10, 15, 17, 25, 48, 65, 77, 124-129, 131
association, 66, 67
Guaranteed increase, 4, 48
Guaranteed,
insurability, 4, 48, 67, 128
issue, 135-137
Guardian, 65

I

Illegal companies, 39, 78, 82-84
Incontestability,
clause, 100
period, 5, 14, 57, 66, 125, 127
Individual Benefits, 185
Individual Retirement Account, *see* IRA
Installment payments, 99
Insurance after diagnosis, 135
Insurers, 12-14, 30, 74, 126, 158
Interest, 17, 18, 67, 69, 123, 150
Investors, 21, 93, 96, 110
IRA, 113-114, 150
Irrevocable beneficiary, 126
IRS, 140

J

John Hancock, 132, 135
Jrnl of the Amer Soc of CLU & ChFC, 76n.10, 79n.14

K

Kansas Business Journal, 75n.7
Kelly, Dr. John, 89-90, 108
see Life Partners, 93

L

Lancaster Annuity Services Co, 83
Lapsed policies,
and reinstatements, 5, 100, 125, 135
Larson, Per, 8n.5, 21, 24, 25n.14, 27, 41, 49n.4, 52, 58, 60, 61, 69, 73, 75
Lazzareschi, Carla, 172
Legacy Benefits, 26,

36, 53, 54, 100, 188
License-pending, 35
Licensing, 19, 71-88
LifeAID, 185
Life Benefactors, 36, 37, 185
Life Entitlements, 34, 50, 63, 66, 72, 73, 186
Life expectancy, 8-10, 14, 17, 18, 20, 28, 36, 56, 61, 63, 68, 74, 78, 81, 82, 130, 131, 135, 140, 165, 170
Life Partners (LPI), 82, 93- 123, 167
    "fractional" interests 98, 112
    mystery owners, 108
    SEC lawsuit, 106
Life Today, 21, 35, 50, 101, 126, 188
Lifetime Funding, 113
Lifetime Options, 62, 186
LifeWise, 165, 187
Lincoln National Life, 13, 90n.13, 98
Living Benefits, 31n.4, 74, 99, 186
Living trust, 153
Loans, 13, 17, 18, 67, 123, 169-171
Los Angeles Times, 171, 172
Low-ball offers, 66

M

Master contract, 6, 125, 127
Maturity value
    disability clause, 75
McCormack, Thomas, 99, 146, 160
McDowell, David, 155, 156
Means-based benefits, 28, 29, 153, 160
Medicaid, 28, 29
Medical Escrow Soc, 82
Medical expenses, 143, 145
Medical records, 25, 42, 58, 60
Medicare, 28
MetLife, 13, 101, 107
Metropolitan Life, 13, 101, 107
Mortgage insurance, 127

N

NAIC, 9, 10, 78, 80, 102
NAPWA, 110-111
Nat Assoc for People with AIDS, 110-111
Nat Assoc Insur Comm (NAIC), 9, 79, 80, 103
National Med Funding, 111, 165, 188
National Viatical Assoc (NVA), 95, 97, 99, 103
National Viator Reps, 48, 55n.1, 189
Needs-based benefits, 28, 29, 160
Negotiations, 46, 53
Newsweek, 88, 90n.21

New York Newsday, 75n.6
Neuma, 55n.3, 186
New England Mutual, 13, 14, 132, 134
New York, 18, 21, 23, 27, 33, 41, 52, 82, 96, 100, 106, 142
New York Times, 108
Nolo Press, 154
Nonforfeiture Options, 100, 123-125
Nonprofit organizations, 41, 85
No Amer Life & Health, 13, 14n.9, 31n.9
No Amer Secur Admin Assoc (NASA), 101
Notarized signatures, 57

O

Offer, 8-10, 17, 23, 30, 43, 47, 53, 59, 61, 65, 131
    in Compromise, 144
Offshore corporation, 108
Ornstein, Leo, SEC atty, 110
Owner, 5, 16, 125
Ownership rights, 4, 5

P

Page & Associates, 27, 36, 62, 109, 187
Paid up insurance, 124
Pardo, Brian, 82, 93-122
    "rogue," 105
    vs. NASA, 101
Partial sale, 11, 16, 20
Pay day, 67
Payment, 81
Pension plans, 151
Peterson, David, 7n.3, 19, 20n.12, 21, 40, 136, 137, 160
Physician, 50, 51, 58, 60, 65, 78
PLWA, 41
Policy holder, owner, 125
Policy lapses, 125
Policy loan *see* loans
Policy size, 11, 20
Pomeroy, Glenn, Sec Comm, N.D., 101
Power of Attorney, 63
POZ, 54n.4
Pre-death benefits, 77 *see* ADB
Premature withdrawals, 150
Premium, 5, 6, 17, 67, 124, 125, 128, 136, 142-143, 145
Premium waiver, 18, 128, 129
Probate, 154, 155
Proof of health, 4, 48
Prudential, 13
Public assistance, 28, 80,160
Purchase price, 60, 61, 75, 166
PWA, 41

Q

Qualified Retirement Trusts (QRT), 150
Questions, 20, 52
Q-Foil Inc, 72
Quinn, Jane B, 86

R

Reduced paid up insurance, 124
Re-entry rates, 129
Referral fees, 51, 67
Registration, 40
Regulation, 71-88
Reinstatements, 125
Renewal rate, 129
Renfrew Financial, 189
Resale, 21, 34, 94
Rescind, 26, 67-69, 80
Reverse mortgage, 169-171
Rosenkrantz, Herbert, 171

S

San Francisco Chron, 38n.4
Scam, 101, 107
Securities Exchange Commission (SEC) 99, 104, 106-110
SGLI, 129
Social Security, 131, 139, 140, 149, 152, 175
    see SSDI, SSI
Sound mind, 63
Special Needs Trust, 153-158
Split policy, 168
SSDI, 28
SSI, 28, 152, 158
State Farm, 13
Sterling Signatures, 112
Sterling Trust, 108, 112
Supplementary Trusts, 154
Surrender form, 16
Surrender policy, 123
Surrender value, 17, 123
Switch-hitters, 34, 35, 96

T

Tax-free, 140, 167
Taxes, 27, 28, 80, 113-114, 139
    EIC, 146
    OIC, 144
Term insurance,
    see group
Texas Monthly, 90
Texas Triangle, The, 102-103
Timing, 47
Tracking viators, 26
Transfer ownership, 4-6, 60, 68, 125
Trusts, 5, 153-155
Two policies, 47

U

Underwriting, 62
    insurance, 66
    legal, 61, 62
    medical, 61
Universal life insur,